WOMEN
& WORK
IN THEIR OWN WORDS
edited by MAUREEN R. MICHELSON

Library telephone #
585 - 7174.

due July 31
due on May 22.

NEWSAGE PRESS

√2/03

DEDICATION

For my daughter, Alexa Ruth, that she may grow up knowing that women's work is all work. And for my Mother, and my Great Aunt Mayme, and all the women who have gone before whose lives have made today's choices possible.

ACKNOWLEDGMENTS

Most importantly, I want to thank the women in this book who shared their lives so openly and courageously. Their stories give me great hope and pride in womanhood. A special thank you to all the photographers whose images appear in this book and their creative talents used to capture these moments in working women's lives.

Special thanks to the following friends and family for their support and encouragement: Rhonda Hughes, Gary Spoerle, Lorraine Michelson, and Suzanne Bronson. For her strong editorial support I want to acknowledge Betty Brickson. And to Michael Dressler for his participation in the first edition of this book in 1986.

Women & Work: In Their Own Words

Copyright 1994 by Maureen R. Michelson

All rights reserved. No part of this book may be reproduced or utilized in any form or by any means without permission in writing from the publisher.

Address inquiries to:
  NewSage Press
  PO Box 607
  Troutdale, OR 97060

Second Edition 1994
ISBN 0-939165-23-6

Designed by Laura Shaw
Cover Design by Adam McIsaac and Laura Shaw
Printed in Korea
Cover Photo Credits: Raisa Fastman (top and right), Cheryl Bray (bottom), and Candace Allen (top left).
Library of Congress Cataloging-in-Publication Data

  Michelson, Maureen R., 1951
  Women & Work: in their own words / by Maureen R. Michelson:

CONTENTS

INTRODUCTION

WOMEN in the work force is a subject that has been analyzed and categorized by countless experts and academicians in numerous books. But rarely are women given the opportunity to speak for themselves, in their own words, about their work and what it means in the context of their lives. For this book, I sought out typical working women from across the United States, although some may be accomplished or noted in their particular field. However, as you will learn from reading about these women's lives, every woman is far from typical in the daily heroics of her life, even though she may never receive a moment's recognition in history.

It is difficult to represent the great variance of work that women do since it would take an encyclopedic effort to show the full spectrum of "women's work," which is essentially all work. Traditional work as well as nontraditional work are included since they are all part of working women's lives in the United States. However, as Kristin Watkins points out in her essay on nontraditional jobs, only a small percentage of women work in nontraditional jobs. And those who do are primarily in professional occupations such as lawyer or doctor. Unfortunately, even though we are fast approaching a new century, change moves slowly in many aspects of nontraditional work for women. Still the number of women working in blue-collar trades and technical occupations remains small—even though a nontraditional job can mean the difference between poverty and economic self-sufficiency.

Most of the women represented in this book were chosen randomly with no criteria for a certain political leaning or level of consciousness regarding women's issues. Each woman was asked to write, as honestly as she could, about herself and her work and the issues that concern her. The door was open for each person to share her reality, whatever it might be. As the stories unfold, common threads reveal themselves as the women talk about family, child care, money, spiritual strength, discrimination, sexual harassment, and the triumphs and hardships of being in a work world that has yet to accept and acknowledge women's full participation. In addition, there is the unique history of each woman, the struggles she faces because of her age, race, sexual preference, physical challenges, or work situation. And there are the successes that result from those struggles. Combined, these stories are powerful reminders that stereotypes—of any kind—are meaningless. Behind the stacks of government statistics on women in the workplace there are human beings, each with a history, each with a story waiting to be told.

The personal experiences shared in *Women & Work: In Their Own Words* quickly cut through the distant, unfeeling, objectifying of the work world. With encouragement, most of the women were able to go beyond the surface niceties and share the harder parts, whether figuring out how to juggle children and work, or facing harassment on the job. However, there are those cautiously stated concerns that belie much deeper stories that, even in the mid-1990s, women still do not feel safe to share. One participant sent a personal note with her statement that read in part, "Unfortunately, I couldn't bring myself to include all the injustices and prejudices I've encountered as an Hispanic female in a white, male-dominated field. I truly love my job and I'm hesitant to injure the tentative respect I've garnered so far." In a phone conversation, another woman told me she was not willing to discuss being a lesbian even though in her college years she was a politically active lesbian. "I'm not out at work. It does not feel safe, especially with my boss."

There is pride and determination in these women's stories that defy turning back or being less than they know they can be. As one young woman so aptly wrote, "We are all conditioned through our adolescence to be 'careful' or 'don't worry, daddy will take care of you' or to 'marry a nice man to support you.' But as an adult woman now, I want to face the world and its problems on my own, using whatever technique it takes to find solutions." And with such determination, many of the women offer inspiration because they persist with their dreams. One independent, small-business owner wrote, "It is not always easy to follow your heart, work in a male-dominated field, and withstand criticism while breaking away from the traditional mold that has been set for women in our society.... My business has brought me a sense of fulfillment, accomplishment, independence, and financial success, which in turn, has built my self-esteem and sense of self-worth." Also, there are stories of courage. Women challenging the establishment when faced with sexism, whether filing lawsuits for denied tenure, challenging unfair work policies, or changing

sexist language in an organization's by-laws. "The victory cost me seven years of struggle but it was well worth it," writes one professor. "The consciousness of the academic community has been raised and many of us are working hard to make it easier for women of all ages to pursue careers in mathematics and science."

Unquestionably, the 1990s is a time of great revolution in the work force, primarily because women are present in unprecedented numbers. Almost half of today's employed in the United States are women, in addition to the millions of unrecognized—and unpaid—women working as homemakers. Many women address social issues, but oftentimes in their own voices with their own experiences. They may not be aware that the statistics say "one-third of all families maintained by women have incomes below the poverty level," but they do say, "It's so difficult to make ends meet." Primary concerns among working women are pay equity and child care. Whether college graduates or high school dropouts, women earn an average of 60 cents for every dollar their male counterparts are paid; a ratio that has existed since 1939. And for minority women, the gap usually deepens even more, and the "glass walls" go even higher. Sumru Erkut discusses these disparities for nontraditional employees in her essay and offers suggestions for change in the business world.

As for child care, more than half of all mothers in this country are working women with more than 12 million children under age 6 (a number greater than the population of New York City). Trying to manage work and child care is a primary concern for working parents. "Breaking away from my image that 'a good mom is a mom who stays home and takes care of her kids' was the most difficult struggle in my transition to be a working mom," admits one woman. "My old belief has been replaced by a new belief that being a great mom is a mom who works and loves her kids as much as any mom can." Nancy L. Marshall's essay, "Having It All," speaks to the difficulties of being a working parent and affirms that it is possible to work and have a family.

There are few work situations women have not at least pioneered. As women move into non-traditional jobs in greater numbers, there are a myriad of issues clouding work relationships between women and men. The concerns vary greatly, from one woman who says "the biggest objection I heard when I was hired was that the men would have to shut the bathroom door," to another who was told flat out that she wouldn't be hired "because you're a woman." Throughout this book many of these issues are talked about, but with the power of the individual experience. Many women have found support and a sense of fairness from male co-workers, breaking ground for mutual respect and friendship on the job. However, harassment still thrives, particularly in nontraditional jobs where women threaten the male status quo. "The territory is clearly marked and gendered by photographs of women in biki-nis in power tools," states one woman in a nontraditional job. "Our tools are called strippers, dykes, pliers. We work with nipples, screws, nuts, cock valves…." Whether faced with a daily bar-rage of sexual innuendoes, or hired for the job—or not hired—based on physical appearance, women have a heightened awareness for identify-ing sexual harassment and its many guises. A musician wrote, "Many of my first jobs were in female bands where looks outweighed musician-ship, and unprofessional treatment and low wages were commonplace…and I was almost fired from a cruise ship job based on the lame excuse that I would have to share a bathroom with the male musicians. I was able to retain the job only after threatening a law suit." The essay by Colleen Phelan on sexual harassment and what to do about it is an essential primer for a working woman in the 1990s.

My hope is that this collection of women's sto-ries, essays, and photographs will offer tomorrow's women the inspiration and courage they need to mold their lives on their terms. That is why this book includes two essays that specifically talk about girls, their self-esteem, and empowerment. Nell Merlino discusses the annual "Take Our Daughters to Work Day" started by the Ms. Foundation for Women as a way for adults to reach out to girls and include them in today's working world so they can plan for tomorrow. On the other hand, the essay by 13-year-old Mavis Gruver, "Girls Empowering Girls," is about girls already taking matters into their own hands. Gru-ver, one of the editors of the girls' magazine, *New Moon*, gives adults a window of insight into the concerns and interests of girls and their dreams for tomorrow.

And for those of us in the midst of our work-ing lives, my hope is that *Women & Work: In Their Own Words* will be an opportunity to take stock of our accomplishments, inspire us to remove barriers facing women, and to hold onto our dreams.

MAUREEN R. MICHELSON
April 1994

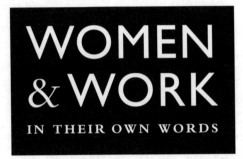

WOMEN & WORK

IN THEIR OWN WORDS

studied already

Maisha Moses, 23, teaches mathematics to junior high school students through the Algebra Project. Moses believes that in the 1990s knowledge of mathematics and science is as important to the freedom of African Americans as access to the vote was in the 1960s.

BOTH OF MY PARENTS were activists in the civil rights movement of the early 1960s. They fought for freedom and equality for black people in this country. When my siblings and I were young, my parents told us of this ongoing struggle and of their experiences in this struggle. In telling us their stories, my parents also told us of their continued dedication and commitment to struggle. As a result, from a very young age, I had a strong desire to do whatever I could to help make things more equal and just for African-American people in this country.

While growing up in Cambridge, Massachusetts, my parents tried to see to it that I was personally sheltered from many racial and social injustices. I was, however, very much aware of them. The most common injustice that I came face-to-face with everyday was education. When I was in eighth grade, my father came into my class to teach me algebra because my school didn't offer it. He worked with me and three other students in the class selected by the teacher who were all white. Because my father had taught me algebra in the eighth grade, I was eligible to take the college preparatory and honors level math and science courses when I got to high school.

Throughout all four years of high school there were only two other black students in some of my math and science courses. They were both male and they were both a year ahead of me. This was in a school where approximately 30 percent of the student body was black.

Many of my friends were placed in general math and science courses. This effectively meant that they were taking courses in the tenth and eleventh grades that I had taken in the eighth and ninth grades. I saw this as an injustice of the system. I felt that the main reason they were in general-level courses and I was in the advanced-level course was not because of any difference in intelligence, but because of injustice in the system. I felt that many students had been, and are being, mis-educated and cheated out of an opportunity to receive the best quality education possible. I was lucky because I had parents who demanded and saw to it that I received an education that they thought I had a right to, and not an education that the system thought I should be satisfied with.

Because of my high school experiences, I became more concerned about issues of equality in education, especially for black children. I saw how education plays such an important role in the decisions young people in this country can make about their lives. When I got to college I worked extensively with young students teaching and tutoring them in mathematics. I also began work with the Algebra Project. My involvement grew out of my father's efforts to teach me algebra in the eighth grade. The project's goal is to

ensure that all students, especially African-American students and other students of color, enter high school with the mathematical preparation to enter into the college preparatory math sequence. The Algebra Project believes that access to algebra and higher-level mathematics is just as important to the freedom of African-American people today as access to the vote was in the 1960s. The current technological revolution demands that people have a level of mathematics and science understanding. Those without it will be locked out from full and equal participation in our economic, political, and social institutions.

The goals, beliefs, and mission of the Algebra Project resonated very strongly with me. When I graduated from college in 1991, I decided that I wanted to work on the Algebra Project full time. It was decided that the best place for me to work was in Oakland, California. Part of me was very nervous because I did not know what to expect. I was leaving all my family and friends to go to the other side of the country, to a place I had never been to before. I had lived the last 15 years in Cambridge, but I was ready for the challenges and changes that a move to Oakland would bring.

At the time, Oakland had only one school, King Estates Junior High School, involved with the Algebra Project. My job was and is to support the teachers in their efforts to implement project curriculum, so I spend most of my time in the classroom working with teachers and students.

One of the challenges I've faced has been learning to work with, and gain the respect of, people who are much older and have much more experience than I do. I have learned that I have knowledge and skills I can contribute and I've also learned the importance of learning from others and respecting their beliefs, opinions, and knowledge.

One of my greatest joys has been working with the students of King Estates who face overwhelming challenges in their personal lives. Many students come to King with deficits in all subject areas and are turned off from school. Yet the more I work with them, the more I see and understand the brilliant minds that many of our students have. Unfortunately, these minds are being mis-educated. I had one student tell me that she was afraid she was getting dumber from year to year because she wasn't being taught properly. These students are virtually powerless to do anything about their feelings. As a result, they act out in unproductive ways. Our children are slowly dying in our schools. It has been very frustrating and painful for me to see this, but it is also a challenge. My joy has been in being able to get to know, and make friends with, many of the students at King Estates. I have learned a great deal from them, and I hope I have been able to teach them a little as well.

Kasey Rose, 25, is in her sixth season working for the federal government parachuting into wilderness areas to fight fires. She is one of only about a dozen women and 400 men who work as smoke jumpers in the western states.

I HAD JUST completed a bicycle trip with five other young women down the Pacific Coast when I heard from a friend that a fire crew he worked with needed someone to fill in. I loaded my bicycle and myself onto the next bus out of LA and headed north, excited at the prospect of new country, people, and experiences.

I first heard about smoke jumping from Moe, a solid, incredibly fit and hard-working woman who was the only woman on the 20-person fire crew. We were lacing up our eight-inch, Vibram-sole work boots one morning when she started talking about smoke jumping. I stared at her in amazement and asked, "They really do that?" She explained about wilderness fires inaccessible by road that smoke jumpers parachuted in to extinguish. I knew this was for me.

That winter, when I was 20, I applied for, and was accepted to, rookie training the following summer. At that time, I was on the rowing crew at the University of Washington so I supplemented my six-day-a-week intense workouts with visits to the varsity weight room pull-up bar. I showed up to rookie training at the smoke jumper base in Redmond, Oregon only one day after rowing with the university's women's junior

varsity eight and winning a gold medal at the collegiate national championships. My biggest apprehension was passing the PT (physical training) test: seven pull-ups, 25 push-ups, 45 sit-ups, and a one-and-a-half mile run timed under 11 minutes. Jet lag and four hours sleep didn't help relax me. The test was the easiest thing I did during my four weeks of rookie training. I never really doubted my ability to make it through training but I remember staggering through the high desert with an 80-pound pack in the swel-

Photo: Jeff Henry

tering sun and thinking, "I'm not having much fun."

When I arrived at my home base in Winthrop, Washington, I realized that my reputation had preceded me. The men had heard that I was a large, strong rower. They gathered that first morning to watch the three new "rooks" do PT and were shocked to see the "bull dyke" swinging a long, blond ponytail and pulling a long, lean, buxom body over the pull bar.

I was told that my rookie year would be tough, both physically and emotionally. My body had never been so broken down. One ridge-top practice jump was followed by a downhill pack-out. With 90 to 100 pounds on my back, even the very first step down the hill was wobbly. I was terrified and I knew I had to complete this test, but each step was unstable. I gulped back tears as I merely balanced my way down. The mental drain was even harder. Even though rookie harassment is a tradition, I remember thinking, "Oh, they'll be nice to me. I'm a nice person." One evening as I sat crying in my room after work, I heard what I realized was my rookie bro crying in his room next door. Even this 195-pound, rugby-playing, ex-Army ranger was pushed to tears.

That year was awfully hard. I questioned myself and wondered if I was really strong enough to be a jumper. But being a smoke jumper has done a number on my own self-concept. Now, I feel I can·do anything if I want to. Anybody can, for that matter. The job itself is truly amazing. The crisp memory of flying over the North Cascades and kneeling in the open door of the airplane (twin-engine Otter) will remain with me forever. My gaze climbs summit

Photo: Jeff Henry

after summit, over glaciers and ice-blue mountain lakes. I feel like the chosen one.

Smoke jumpers as a group are very competitive. The guys always invent little challenges—who can do the most pull-ups, do the rope climb the fastest, turn off his watch alarm first. I kept up and some men found that threatening. One time, on a six-mile packout, I dropped behind to help another jumper adjust her pack. I walked with her for awhile but I was tormented by the image of "the two girls" coming in last. I asked her if she minded if I forged on ahead and she encouraged me to "go get 'em!" I practically ran down the trail, bent over from the weight of my pack—my back, legs, shoulders, feet, *everything* burning with fatigue. I finally overtook the six men who had stopped to rest in the shade along the trail. At the sight of me, one of the more insecure fellows jumped up as though to push on ahead of me, but he caught himself and tried to act cool by fiddling with his pack. I greeted them and walked on by to be the first one to the trailhead. In retrospect, I would have liked to stop and rest with the guys, but I was too competitive.

There have been times when I questioned whether I should be in the job since I was breaking down traditions: the boys' club. Often the men laughed and joked in a manner I could not be a part of and I wondered, "What am I doing here? I don't belong." But then I might share a personal conversation with a jumper who opens up to me because I *am* a woman. Or I will jump into a flower-covered alpine meadow overlooking a glacier-fed lake and my passion for my job overrides the doubt. I know I can be a smoke jumper, too.

I thought I might jump for a couple of years to put myself through college and then I get on with a "real life." I graduated from the university three years ago and I'm still planning to jump again this summer. In discovering the world of seasonal work, I have learned that I like it. A summer full of intensive traveling, working, and saving money balances nicely with a fall learning to surf in Baja and the rest of the winter spent on the slopes in northern Idaho. We joke about getting "real jobs" some day, but we love what we do and the options are endless.

Yiu Hai Quon, 97, owns the Grand Star Restaurant in Chinatown in Los Angeles. Lovingly referred to as "Mama Quon" by her customers and family, she continues to cook in her restaurant, health permitting.

I WAS BORN Yiu Hai Seto in Hoiping, China, in 1899. I am now 97 years young. Until I fell and broke my hip last year, I worked as a cook at the restaurant. I cook there everyday, and people in Chinatown know me as "Mama Quon." I love cooking, something I've done for a long time, and will be doing again when I'm better. I still visit the restaurant once or twice weekly because I like it there and people keep asking for "Mama."

When I was a young girl in China, my parents taught me to cook. I cooked for my father's 60 to 100 produce workers; that's how I got started. I was my father's favorite, and he would not allow the family to bind my feet, but I remember when my sister and I had to hide under the bed for a couple of months to escape this practice.

When I was 9, professional matchmakers arranged an engagement to a 12-year-old boy from Los Angeles. At 16, I married Him Gin Quon, and came to the United States in 1922. I was one of only about 11 Chinese women in Chinatown. Life was hard and times were rough. Sorting walnuts at home into seven grades, at six cents a pound, was one of the jobs available to women. For seven years I sorted walnuts till 3 a.m. while carrying my children on my back.

In 1931, I began working in my father-in-law's restaurant, washing dishes and vegetables. Most of the patrons were Chinese, but non-Chinese also came to eat. Sometimes they refused to pay afterwards, fights would occur, people were pushed down the stairs, heads were broken. There was prejudice, intimidation, and violence in those early days.

In 1932 I went back to China with my husband and nine children. We farmed and lived there for about eight years. When war broke out and the Japanese bombed our village, we decided to return to the US. En route to Hong Kong, our junk was strafed and it sank. The gold that I had hidden in my money belt kept us alive for two years in Hong Kong while we waited for passage to California. This was around 1940.

In 1950 we opened the Grand Star Restaurant where I cooked every day. Things are so much easier now. In the early days, if someone ordered chicken, I'd have to kill it myself and prepare it. Now meat comes dressed, cleaned, cut, and ready for cooking. I enjoy being a cook and am waiting to get back to it. Meanwhile, I'm working with doctors and physical therapists to recover from my operation. I also spend time with my 9 children, 26 grandchildren, and 13 great-grandchildren.

15

Alice Villalobos, 47, is a veterinarian specializing in the treatment and clinical research of cancer in pet animals. She is the founder of Coast Pet Clinic, and Animal Cancer Clinic, which is the biggest veterinary hospital in the world owned by a woman.

I WAS EITHER going to be a nun or a veterinarian since the third grade, but there were no convents offering veterinary medical training. After graduation from an all-girl, Catholic high school, I chose to pursue my scientific career as a worldly individual, attending a local community college in the South Bay of Los Angeles, then a state university, and finally, the University of California at Davis. I remember each step of the way as a struggle with great personal rewards. Very few counselors, family members, or teachers really encouraged me at the beginning and I don't blame them. Truly, getting into UC Davis vet school in 1966, 1967, and 1968 was a chance of 12.5 to 1—and worse for females! It took me three applications to get in.

It was harder preparing and trying to get into vet school than being in it. One problem was money. Once I got in, the health profession loans were forthcoming. Being number four in a family of five children, with my dad working in a factory all his life for $6,000 a year and just being laid off, wasn't exactly promising for my destiny! Everyone started to believe in me once I got into veterinary school.

Life has continued to be a struggle with great personal rewards on a daily basis because I'm not practicing general veterinary medicine as most members of my profession do. Early on in my career, I decided to specialize in cancer therapy for pets. This obsession lead to the start of my own clinic in order to have the freedom of a 45-minute office call, rather than the routine 10-to-15-minute type. Now, apparently I have ownership of probably the largest veterinary facility owned by a "single woman," as the law states it.

I've been involved in the field of cancer research for 24 years. I'm considered a grandmother in the field and a world-renowned expert in the treatment of pets with cancer and related diseases such as feline leukemia and immunodeficiency viruses. My message to the world is that pets can survive (cancervive) cancer if we challenge the disease. The warning signs of cancer and illness in pets need early, expert attention in order to win the battle. Perhaps some of the methods we use to treat animals now may be acceptable for people in the future.

Among our patients are "victims of a cement society." Concrete is encroaching on wilderness animals such as the possum who gets hit by a car. We provide medical care for homeless, wild, injured, or sick animals through a fund set up to accept donations from the kindhearted and from our hospital that directs all fees for euthanasia towards the fund. Besides caring for cancer patients referred to our service from veterinarians all over southern California, we place 250 to 300 kittens and aid about 175 birds and other miscellaneous animals on a yearly basis. Our service has helped over 7,000 animals.

Every day has its struggles. My biggest headache is the responsibility of keeping a service-oriented business operational. Preserving the love relationship that forms between people and pets is where my heart is and just a sincere "thank you, doc" for helping "my little pal" is our reward.

These struggles continue into life's everyday storms, like negotiating my career through marriage, sports injuries, illness, fundraisers, and burn out, as well as those of my staff, family, and friends. It's no picnic making payroll for a large staff and maintaining the helm of a service organization over dangerous recession waters, not withstanding the LA traffic, riots, fires, earthquakes, and floods!

By 1990 our staff grew to a total of 70 hardworking, pet-care professionals with an intern class and clinical staff totaling 12 veterinarians—until the recession hit, and hit, and continued to hit. Well-intended people asked us to give them a break when treating their pets, then they slowly paid or didn't pay. This put us into a recession-related cash flow problem while the prices of drugs, supplies, labor, and workman's compensation just kept going up. Thanks to the clear-minded, patient skills of our hospital administrator, we got back on track. The clinic and cancer center have endured the rough waters of recession. Our experience gives us the wisdom and power to continue doing what we love the most—taking care of man's best friend.

Photo: Brad Graverson

REHABILITATION NURSE

Susie Matz, 48, is a registered nurse working for the past 16 years in a hospital, primarily in rehabilitation.

I WAS TO GRADUATE from nursing school in 1968 and marry when an airplane crash created my soul's biggest challenge. Waking up in the airplane, I knew I was a paraplegic. I couldn't feel anything from the waist down. There was no conceivable way I knew how I was going to live this way, and I wanted to die. At 22 years of age, I was already angry, misread from my childhood, and in the middle of two brothers with whom I couldn't compete. Now I was faced with no control over bowel and bladder functioning, no more orgasms, atrophying muscles, physical inability. Being catapulted from a dysfunctional family into this cataclysmic catastrophe was just too much to cope with.

Sadness and depression set in, I couldn't face a soul—I would not go out of the house. How was an ordinary person with a low self-esteem going to survive? Now came the challenge; to sink or swim. Piloted and driven by anger and rage, the purpose of my destiny drove me to swim, and I now realize that I had the inner gift of God's love and the power of the Universe that I could access and use.

Grudgingly, I learned how to control my body and get around in a wheelchair. I went back to school, finished my education as an RN [registered nurse] and tried passing the boards. I failed. Years later I tried the LVN [licensed vocational

nurse] boards and passed. No one would hire me as an LVN, so I sat on the bed with all the textbooks from school and read and read. Six hours a day for six months. I retook the RN test. I did it. I passed!

Getting a job was the next hurdle. They all said, "You can't do the physical things required by a nurse from a wheelchair." Finally, a CETA program [Comprehensive Employment Training Act] opened at a hospital near my home. After two years of fruitless hunting, a job! "Come to work on Monday," they said on the phone. "You're going to be a patient representative." I knew what it was like to be a patient, now I had to learn the hospital administrative side of things to balance my perspective.

Two years later, the discharge coordinator job in the rehab center opened, and I was going to where I belonged—helping people with disabilities get a start on their new way of life. My job is to insure when patients are discharged, that they and their families have been educated about their disability. What I learned for myself and for my patients is that self-advocacy is the only answer. No one in the world knows your particular situation—your thoughts, feelings, desires, and dreams. We each need to realize that the true measure of self-esteem is listening to your own inner voice and acting on it. If a patient can come away with this knowledge, I feel I have been successful.

I have always felt I shouldn't be real vocal because I don't represent all handicapped people. On the other hand, I have found health care pro-

Photo: Jeff Share

fessionals have poor insight into the care and lifestyle of a person with my problem. Reality orientation is difficult and often the staff tries to ignore me by treating me like a patient. They can't ignore me, you see, I'm one of them. Hopefully, the patients can see me come to work and realize there is life after disability.

I have found strengths in myself I never knew I had. My hope is to touch souls with others; to focus on the strengths, abilities, and love in myself and in others. I used to think I could empower patients to find their own inner strength. I now believe that empowerment comes from within and in reality, I had to find my own first. Having found my own self-empowerment was a witness to people so they could begin to look within themselves for their own.

It is an honor and a privilege to open the door each morning and see the sunshine on the flowers, to be able to get my chair in the car and drive to work. The patients at work are facing what I faced 26 years ago. To put a song in their hearts and hope in their souls, that's the goal. My self-esteem is walking again! No one could tell me I had any exceptional qualities, the wheelchair proved me wrong. I had to come to the test or sit in my room and wither. My hope for others is that they don't wait for a personal tragedy to lift the skin and look within.

Maureen Spencer Forrest, 47, spent 20 years as a police officer in New York before becoming an investigator for the New York City School District. Forrest supervises a team that investigates allegations of child sexual abuse when the accused is an employee of the Board of Education.

IN 1968, I was among the women who took the last "police woman's" examination in New York. From then on, there would be one police officer's test, rather than separate tests for men and women. The separate Police Woman's Bureau would eventually be a thing of the past. I had taken the test at the urging of my father who was a 23-year veteran of the same police force. At the time I took the test I was in college, recently separated from my husband, and the sole support of two children. I never really thought that I would go into the police department. I was an anthropology major and certainly never thought that police work would be a long-term career for me. Actually, I planned to stay for about five years and then go to graduate school.

At the point when I was called to be investigated for entry into the department, which was not until 1973, I had just graduated from college. Employment won out over graduate school. When I did enter the police academy it was apparent that the department was not ready to handle the idea of women working side by side with men on patrol. Even basic things such as uniforms were a challenge. As a matter of fact, we didn't know from day to day what our uniform would be. Skirts? Pants? Actually, it was potluck for a few months. I remember one of my first uniformed assignments was in a high school as a liaison officer. While walking through the hallways I wore the regular patrol officer's uniform with the exception of the pants. The pants were corduroy. One of the teachers approached me wondering what play I was rehearsing for, even though I had my gunbelt and gun slung over my hips.

The reality of seeing women actually walking a beat, riding in a radio car, and performing all the various police functions was not always amusing. There was, at times, vocal and hostile resistance. Male police officers were not always the most hostile. The wives of police officers formed a movement and demonstrated to prevent women from sitting in a radio car with their husbands for eight hours a day. The cry was always that women were not up to the task of being equal partners with the men and their safety was at stake. When I was eventually assigned to my field training officer I was introduced to a gung-ho, ex-marine who always wore military-issue parachute jump boots. On our first night on patrol he was very up-front with his feelings. He didn't think that women belonged "on the job," but he taught me what I needed to know. I told him that I didn't want any special treatment. I just wanted to learn my job. Well, he was a great teacher and I guess I was a good student. When my six months with him were up he told me that I was going to be a good cop—something that every rookie wants to hear.

I tried not to let any naysayers or negative ideas influence me while I was at work. That wasn't always possible for me, being a single parent. There were many times when I reluctantly had to leave and go to work even though my son or daughter was sick. There were days when I just couldn't make a school program or event. But on the other hand, as my assignments changed, so did my flexibility. It was my family, especially my parents, who provided much-needed backup and support. Knowing that my children were safe made it a lot easier to keep my mind where it needed to be when I was at work. And going home to those two bundles of energy certainly reminded me, daily, what was most important to me.

I spent the next 20 years in a variety of assignments. They varied from undercover assignments, hostage negotiation, plainclothes street crime assignments, and working in the district attorney's office investigating felony sex crimes. I have always enjoyed the challenges that law enforcement has presented. Although I have retired from the police force, I have moved on to another investigative agency. This agency conducts investigations of corruption and criminality by school personnel. Currently, I am a confidential investigator supervising a team that investigates allegations of child sexual abuse when the accused is an employee of the Board of Education.

About halfway through my police career, I managed to meet a wonderful man and remarry. We blended our two families and together raised four children. All are a source of great pride and

at least as challenging as my career. Looking back over the years, there were times when I asked myself, "What am I doing here?" There were times when I was confused by the violence that I've witnessed people inflict on one another, and times when I've been scared by some of the situations I've found myself in. But I balance that with the long list of great men and women I have worked with, the experiences I've had that I wouldn't trade for anything, and my ever-present belief that public service and the attempt to work toward society's betterment is gratifying and worthwhile.

Photo: CarolAnn Hawkins

Allison Adler, 26, is the story editor for a one-hour drama series for MTV. In addition to working in an office, she often works from home or at the local coffee house.

I WAS 8, 9, 10; it didn't matter—it was something to set my watch by. I was plugged into the TV. A tin of chocolate cake by my side, I sat bent, concentrated, glued every Sunday morning.

My father, dressed in his mismatched worst, was setting off for his round of golf. He'd poke his head in and shake it in astonishment. Why did this continue to surprise him? "How can you waste a beautiful day watching TV?" he'd ask. I'd give him the same answer, but he always listened as if hearing for the first time. "I'm busy," I'd say, wiping the sleep from my eyes.

A round of golf takes a while and he'd come home, spent and sweaty, smelling of sweet grass and expensive cigars. He'd poke his head back in. I might've been working on a box of Frosted Flakes at this point. "You're in exactly the same place as I left you. You haven't moved. Whatta waste of a day." I'd shrug, flip the channel and he'd shake his head again and trudge off to the shower.

Watching TV wasn't a waste of my time, it was research. My father should have trusted me. I parlayed my bad habit into a career. If only coffee drinking and smoking cigarettes paid as well.

When I graduated from UCLA in 1990 with a degree in creative writing, I was faced with the reality of having to feed myself with my words. It gave a whole new meaning to the phrase, "eating your words." I wrote a couple of spec "thirtysomethings" and got an agent. I took a day job, hoping it wouldn't have to last very long and luckily, it didn't. I was asked to freelance several episodes of "Beverly Hills, 90210" and suddenly words I typed were buying me things. I bought a desk and a new computer; I was purchasing things with the tangible. It felt great. And the first job led into this one. I'm the story editor on the new drama show for MTV. But it's not always easy. The traditional fast-paced style of the network is also emulated behind the scenes. Everything is done as best as possible and in the shortest time imaginable. Just looking forward to a bath at the end of the day sometimes gets me through it.

Writing for television is taking my personal adventures and altering them slightly, standing back and watching. My confrontation with a cable repair person or a dental hygienist can be seen on TV a short time later. I am making my memories concrete. But there are heavy responsibilities sharing my experiences with the crowd. They'd better be interesting or they'll be given re-write. It's not only my head being considered here. There are executive producers, line producers, executives in charge of the production, network people, props, gaffers—the testosterone swirls in gales. All these people can change what had originally been my experience. It's like a game of "operator" at an eighth-grade slumber party. The memory gets more frayed with each sharing, almost threadbare by its air date.

Photo: Theodora Litsios

But, every Sunday, I'm still plugged into the TV. Sure, there have been changes. The set is bigger now, comes in stereo and Spanish simulcast. And I've sworn off chocolate cake—too tough on the thighs. But, hey, Frosted Flakes are a pretty good compromise. And when my father calls me on Sunday, interrupting my research, I can almost hear him smiling proudly on the other side. He trusts me.

Donna Jean Ventresco, 50, has been working for a coal company in Pennsylvania for the past 15 years. She is one of three female coal miners at a company with about 100 miners.

I **GREW UP** with coal mine talkers. My father started when he was 14 and was a miner for 46 years. And my uncles worked there and I guess you could say their talking about it made me go for the job when I got older. I worked two weeks before my mother found out. She wasn't too happy with the fact that I was in the mines. She said that was no place for women. After 15 years, she still isn't too happy with my job. My mother's 83 now, and she says, "Your job is too hard of work for anyone. That's what killed your dad at an early age. He just worked himself to death." My husband, Chuck, a truck driver, was worried about me for a long time. But once I told him that I'm not scared to enter the mines, he stuck right by me.

I had been out of a job for six months when I got the job at the mines. Before that, I made minimum wage at a drapery factory. I bugged a superintendent at the coal company for a year before I got the job, but I was going to get in them mines. He kicked me out of his office a few times. He probably said, "Hire her, and hire her at another mine because I don't want to see her." Two of my friends said, "Women don't belong in the mines. You'll never make it, Jean." So I said, "Yes I will. If it kills me, I'll make it."

Well, I'll tell you about the mines. At first, I was scared that I wouldn't be able to do the work. But once I really got to understand and operate the machines, it made it a lot easier. I don't hate my job at all. I get along real good with everyone, and when you've been through strikes and other hard times, you get to know people. But when I first started working in the mines, you name it, the men said it. They said, "You're a woman, we're gonna have to do the work for you." But after I started working with them, there's no problem, once I proved myself. Now the crew and I all joke around and that really helps a lot. It makes the shift go faster and the work a lot easier. It's like we all stick together.

We just ended a seven-month strike that gave us an hourly raise of $1.30 and job security. Now I make a little more than $17 an hour. The mon-

Photo: Andy Starnes

ey and the benefits are too good to let go of and that helps me keep going. My work includes running the "scoop," a machine that hauls supplies and picks up loose coal; operating a shuttle car for transporting coal; helping to install 18-foot wooden beams to support the roof; and helping the bolter. The hard part at the end of the shift is climbing 200 steps to get out of the mines… you're real tired at the end of the day. My worst experience in the mines was when a rock had fallen on a crew member and the men lifted the rock and I pulled him out from underneath it. He died two days later. It had me shocked up for awhile.

My dreams since I was 16 years old were to have a good husband, children, own my house, and have a Corvette. Well, since then I got all of those things and I'm very happy with my life. I'm a mother of five children from the ages of 26 years through 32 years, and a grandmother of five. I got custody of my first grandson when he was three years old, and he is 15 years old now. It was like starting over after I raised all five of mine, but he's worth it. I want to put in five more years, if possible, on my job. Then hospitalization for me and my husband will be paid for life. I really want that.

Evelyn Irizarry, 52, is principal of an inner-city elementary school in Hartford, Connecticut, and has been in the education field for 20 years.

AFTER GRADUATING from Washington Irving High School in New York City back in 1960, I decided I wanted to be an accountant since mathematics was my "forte." At the time, I did not have the money to go to college so I got a job as a secretary at the Park Royal Hotel with the idea of saving enough money for at least the first semester. But in the meantime, my parents decided to move back to Puerto Rico. I had no choice but to go with them since they would not allow me to remain on my own. I come from a family of four sisters and four brothers, and we all went back to Puerto Rico.

I attended Catholic University of Puerto Rico in my hometown of Ponce. I had saved enough money for that first semester and indicated on my application that I wanted to major in accounting. I also applied for financial aid which was approved for my sophomore year. I had an uncle, an elementary school teacher, who offered me the money on one condition: major in education and become a teacher. Reluctantly, I agreed.

I graduated and taught English in Ponce for two years, but the salary was only $250 a month. I was offered a job with Pan Am World Airways, which would be exciting and double the salary. For a year and a half I worked in San Juan, but there was something missing. I really wasn't feel-

ing good about my job. I didn't feel that what I was doing would eventually make a difference in anyone's life. I quit my job and went back to teaching while attending college on a part-time basis, taking graduate courses. I slept better after that, although most of the time I was exhausted.

I have been in the educational field since then and have never regretted being an educator. Sixteen years ago I was recruited from Puerto Rico because the Hartford school system needed Hispanic administrators. Since then, I have been an English teacher, English chairperson, vice-principal at the high school and middle-school levels, and now a principal of an elementary school. The student population is now approximately 77 percent Puerto Rican and 23 percent black. My job requires firmness, but also flexibility. I must be strict with my students, but also nurturing and caring. I believe in "tough love." I always make sure my students leave my office knowing I disapprove of the *action*, not the *person*. The kids are beautiful; emotional, honest, sensitive, and appreciative. It is the adults' attitude that I find challenging and at times questionable.

Sometimes I say to myself, "My God, I can make a difference between good and bad in that child's life. I have something to do with that little person's total formation as a human being. That's power." Kids need structure, but they need an equal dosage of nurturing and love. We all have strengths and weaknesses; I build on the strengths or successes and not the other way around.

Breaking into the teaching field was easy;

becoming a school principal was not. Discrimination? Sure! It was always there and it will always be there. We all discriminate. Some more than others. We discriminate when we choose our friends; when we judge others without having all the facts. I have felt discrimination since childhood back in New York City. I'm talking about racial discrimination, gender discrimination, and so on. Because I am a woman, a Puerto Rican woman, I find myself constantly proving my capabilities as an administrator. The mentality in my field has always been one where female teachers belong in the classroom and not in an administrative capacity. Some time ago I applied for a principalship and did not get the position *because* I am an Hispanic. The school already had an Hispanic administrator and already had met the quota. The second time around I was not selected because I am a woman. The general feeling was that the position required the "physical strength" and "power" of a man. Some people believe that a male principal will be well respected but not a female principal. Naturally, I was not told that these were the reasons, but I can certainly read between the lines. It is my firm belief that as a Puerto Rican female principal I have to be *twice* as effective as any white-male principal, and also *twice* the educational leader. But I accept the challenge because I am a risk taker.

There have been many rewards during my career, not so much plaques or recognition, but smiling faces. Kids who were my students come back years later with college degrees, a family of their own, a good job. That smile and a "thank you" is all the reward I need.

Photo: Gale Zucker

Abby Abinanti, 46, Yurok, has worked as a lawyer in private practice and public interest law. She is currently Legal Director and Director of the Lesbian of Color Project of the National Center for Lesbian Rights, as well as teaching a class on Federal Indian Law at Stanford Law School.

THERE CAME A TIME when I agreed to it, but I never really wanted to be a lawyer. In 1970 when I was graduating from college, the Bureau of Indian Affairs announced a scholarship program. At that time nationally, only a handful of Indian people had become lawyers, and many of them were not "Indian" identified in their work. The importance of lawyers to my community was emphasized to me by the older women. They understood our increasing need to look to the courts to protect our rights against encroachment—hunting, fishing, territorial, etc., and to enforce promises given at an earlier time when the "value" of those promises was not "understood." They wanted Indian lawyers for the fight. I was one of the few people graduating from our area, and since a college degree was a prerequisite to law school, I was elected. I agreed, because in fact there appeared to be, in the face of their insistence, no good reason not to go.

After graduating from college, I went off to a summer session for Indians designed to prepare us for law school. Unfortunately, no one prepared the law schools for us. After summering in a very supportive academic program we returned to our respective home states to begin law school. In my school one other Indian was enrolled, some schools had two or three. I, along with my two best friends from summer school in two different states, were asked to leave law school. They cited a combination of academic and "attitude" problems. They didn't like us not being like them and we didn't like them not liking us for not being like them. Not a good combination. I realize now from this distance a little coalition building might have prevented some of my anguish, but I had yet to discover that art form. Instead, I returned to the University of New Mexico School of Law, which admitted me in my second year. I finished at New Mexico, supported by an administration that believed Indian people should have Indian lawyers and who weren't offended by my not fitting the image of a law student.

There has been trouble in all of these years. People did not like or accept the idea of Indians or women being lawyers. Some people could not decide which idea they hated more. Some pretended that it didn't make any difference, that we were all the same. I, too, could be "one of the boys," "one of the white boys." Not likely. Both approaches created problems for me. These problems were overlaid by the gap in my experience/reality that, though I was technically a "lawyer," law school actually had not made me into a working lawyer. I *became* a lawyer. I have helped; I have made a difference, a couple of times in a big way, mostly in a small way. I learned that I have a role that includes being responsible for provision of legal services, but not as a leader. I am part of a community, a culture that needs me to do my job, and that other people will do theirs and a whole will be created. I am at peace now with being a lawyer.

In recent years I devoted a majority of my time to work in the juvenile dependency court of San Francisco, targeting Indian Child Welfare Act cases and teaching tribal people involved in tribal courts. Then in late 1992 I decided to return full time to public interest law and accepted the positions at the National Center for Lesbian Rights. I am also teaching Federal Indian Law at Stanford Law School.

Through my work at the center I find myself involved in a movement that is struggling to give meaning to minority involvement, diversity, people of color inclusion, and cultural diversity. The lesbian and gay civil rights movement is gathering momentum in the 1990s, but has not escaped the shortcomings of marginalizing those who are not white males. Participation in leadership of the major national organizations is strikingly white. This is wrong and I hope it changes or it will not really be a movement but a club. It is the most difficult of things to give up privilege fought for or given. I understand but do not accept the results.

Now I am the co-parent of a 2-year old, two cats, and two dogs. My life is different from ten years ago. I am happier, more content, I am a good, solid lawyer and teacher. I have loving friendships. I love my partner and our child, I am proud to be a Yurok, and I am proud of the tribal people of all countries who struggle for cultural survival. And I am grateful to the Old Lady and her family who have sheltered me all these years.

Photo: Nita Winter

Susan Bernadette Pedrick, 27, is a medical records clerk at a hospital.

WRITING ABOUT my employment is no small can of worms. In order to appreciate how I pay rent, an explanation of the events leading to my job would be very important to begin with. The saga of my employment begins when I was fresh out of high school and a girls' group home, and I was hired by the phone company as a directory assistance operator. For two-and-a-half years I endured the purgatory of giving out 900 telephone numbers a day until I was graciously granted a transfer to plant services where I stayed five years.

It doesn't really matter what I did or where I worked, what matters is that everywhere I went, people rather enthusiastically liked or disliked me. That, and the fact that my lifestyle changed drastically to a degree that profoundly affected its end. In short, I started using a lot of drugs. Eventually, the phone company reminded me that I was not the same person they had hired five years previously and invited me to leave, which I did without a fight. I forgive myself for this and don't regret it mainly because I needed to get a lot of things out of my system. Also, it was becoming increasingly more difficult to integrate with a full-time job in an environment such as the one with a large utility company.

Painful and dark things led to two incarcerations and three trips to the hospital. However, at the end of a year I had enough. I had created as many creepy environments and contrived as many paradoxically unfortunate circumstances for myself as I was ultimately capable of producing or enduring. I decided to start putting one foot in front of the other and dig myself out of the hole I had taken such care to prepare.

So, when I was 24-years old I started working as a temporary with an agency. My typing skills were not exactly impeccable, so it was desperately long before the agency found me an assignment. I was the sort of "temp" whose entire income consisted of whatever the agency could come up with for me, and after about a week-and-a-half without work, I panicked. I looked into being a leaflet distributor and ended up enduring seven hours on a truck and managed to earn all of $7.50.

On days that my agency didn't have work for me, I often dressed anyway and went down in person which, if nothing else, certainly left the agency with an impression of me as a motivated, dependable person. Finally, one Friday afternoon it was getting down to the wire on whether or not the agency would have work for me Monday morning. At long last they called and said they had an assignment, but apologized because it was not downtown. It turned out to be working at a hospital eight blocks from where I live!

When I got to the hospital, I encountered an environment that seemed as though if I were ambitious enough it could turn into permanent work. I think I was making $5.50 an hour, which was peak for me. I was thrilled, and I worked very

hard making sure the powers that be were aware of this. I found myself surrounded by people who complained constantly, which appalled me because a large percentage of them were making nearly twice as much as I had struggled to make at other jobs. About four months into my assignment, I was offered a full-time job that meant an instant $500 a month raise with benefits.

In short, considering that I had gone as far as entering amateur stripping contests in nude theaters—and winning them—I'd have to say the thing I like most about my job is having it. Other than that, I appreciate working for a hospital and not a utility or oil company. I thoroughly enjoy being on the positive end and helping people who are in real and dire need of the services I provide. I may only be in medical records, but sometimes what I can do for people is almost as beneficial to them as anything a doctor could do and I am very thankful that I accidentally wound up in such an uplifting context.

On the other hand, I envy the people who were getting a college education while I really had no choice but to fight an exhausting war between my ears as a result of a history that is a little more colorful than I care for it to have been. So, my pet peeve is the fate of being bossed around by people of questionable intelligence simply because they were able to get credentials while I was forced to clean up a mess I didn't make. But I am closer than ever to winning that war and cleaning up that mess. In fact, I may be about to flip the switch from a career of trying to stay out of trouble to getting my first promotion. Wish me luck.

WHY TAKE OUR DAUGHTERS TO WORK

NELL MERLINO

IN EARLY 1991, Marie C. Wilson, president of the Ms. Foundation for Women began gathering disturbing statistics that demonstrated that adolescence was taking a greater toll on the self-esteem of America's adolescent girls than boys. As an activist leader of an organization that has played an intimate role in the lives of countless women, Wilson suspected as much. She had seen the impact of adolescence arrive all too reliably for girls—loss of confidence, shyness, negative body image, eating disorders, teen pregnancy, poverty, discrimination, and substance and sexual abuse.

Intent on interrupting this viscious cycle, and supporting girls' self-esteem, Wilson and Idelisse Malave, vice president of the Ms. Foundation, created the National Girls Initiative. For the next two years they and the initiative's coordinator, Kristen Golden, convened groups of women and girls to test programs and identify solutions. Feeling that a visible national public education effort was essential, they called me in to review two years' worth of findings, and from our discussions emerged Take Our Daughters to Work Day.

In creating Take Our Daughters to Work Day, I was struck by a University of Minnesota finding about the significant difference one caring adult could make in a girl's life. Shortly thereafter, I attended my father's retirement dinner and recalled how I had accompanied him to work as a girl and how that experience had informed and inspired me. I felt asking people to take the girls in their lives to work—at an office or at home—could produce personal alliances for girls and also heighten institutional awareness.

The idea was that one day a year, every daughter would be encouraged to enter the working world and witness firsthand the incredible range of career opportunities available. Girls would observe their mothers and other women working in hospitals, foundries, law firms, restaurants, government offices, television studios, police departments, factories, laboratories, and thousands of other employment situations. On this day, daughters guided by parents would get a glimpse of the challenges and opportunities that lie ahead. Wilson, Malave, Golden, and I were excited by the prospect of turning a spotlight on the concerns of girls, and we resolved to implement it as a pilot

Photo: Cherry Kim

program in New York City.

The public was first introduced to Take Our Daughters to Work Day through a short column in *Parade* magazine in May 1992. About a month before, Gloria Steinem, the co-founder of *Ms.* magazine, and Walter Anderson, the editor of *Parade*, met for lunch in a New York restaurant. During their conversation, Steinem described plans for a day when individuals, companies, and organizations would share their workday with girls, ages 9 to 15, so that girls could experience the working world and the work force could get a good look at its future employees and employers.

The *Parade* article, which reached over 70 million readers, ensured that Take Our Daughters to Work Day would not be restricted to New York. The article prompted thousands of mothers, fathers, and grandparents to put down their newspapers that Sunday morning and write to an organization that most of them had never heard of. The letters expressed support for an organization committed to projects and policies that promote a world peopled evenly with diverse and economically empowered women and men. Many parents expressed concerns that their daughters lacked self-confidence, clear goals, and hope for the future. Without a chance to see the variety of careers that are available to women, parents feared their daughters would fall into traditional roles and limited job opportunities.

The parents' letters echoed the findings of Dr. Gilligan and the Harvard project. By surveying girls ages 7 to 17 and listening to them as authorities on their own experiences, the Harvard researchers found that adolescence is a critical turning point in a woman's development. During the transition from childhood to womanhood, girls hear conflicting messages in school, through the mass media, and by watching their mothers negotiate in the world of work and family. Girls begin to understand the limits imposed on women in a society dominated by white males. They tend to internalize their confusion and frustration, which leads to a decline in self-esteem and a loss of confidence and voice.

Another poll by the American Association of University Women confirmed that there is a significant gender gap in self-esteem among adolescent girls and boys. The 1990 survey of 3,000 youngsters between grades four and ten found that in elementary school, 60 percent of girls and 67 percent of boys were happy with themselves. By high school, however, only 29 percent of girls said they were happy with themselves, compared to 46 percent of boys. The study also found a strong correlation among competence in math and science, adolescent self-esteem, and career aspirations.

After reading the *Parade* article, one mother wrote: "I have a 21-year-old daughter who would have benefited from this program, had it been offered several years ago when she was at that impressionable age. She grew up with no clear idea of what she wanted to do when she finished school. I did what I could as a single parent raising her and my son with limited funds and little extended family support, and her self-esteem is not what it should be. She became a single mother four months after she graduated from high school and had a second child 15 months later. Neither of the fathers of her children have been supportive. She's been on welfare since she graduated—any parent's nightmare.

"I've worked for over 13 years as a secretary for one of the largest employers in Washington State. Though it was never my ambition to be a secretary, it put food on my children's table and kept a roof over their heads. I wouldn't particularly wish this on my daughter, but there are many different types of jobs in my company. If (girls) could be exposed to different jobs within a company for a day, it might plant a seed."

Approximately one million girls from throughout the nation participated in the first Take Our Daughters to Work Day on April 28, 1993. When parents were unable to take their own daughters to work, friends, neighbors, and organizations stepped in. The Girl Scouts of the USA, the YWCA, and other groups helped match girls with workers, as well as publicize events. The New York City public school system placed over 2,000 ninth-grade girls with participating businesses. Companies, government agencies, schools, and institutions opened their doors to tomorrow's working women.

From this auspicious beginning, the program grew. In 1994, millions more girls participated and similar programs emerged in England, Japan, Puerto Rico, and Guam. To promote the Take Our Daughters to Work philosophy year-round, clubs formed in major cities, such as Boston and Chicago. The 1994 event even encompassed adolescent boys, taking them to child care centers and nursing homes in their communities. While girls were out exploring the public arena of work that has so long been closed to women, boys were encouraged to visit the more private worlds of family and caring which they don't traditionally frequent. The goal: a society where men and women perform together the equally rigorous work of wage earning and caretaking, where women and men are comfortable at both.

For many parents, the thought of taking their daughters to work was like showing them the dark side of the moon. But as a result of this national effort they soon recognized that all they needed to do was tell their daughters about how they got their jobs, what they did to put food on the table, how they ran the house, where they went during the day and why. The event also offered parents an opportunity to explain the lifestyle choices they made and discuss whether they are happy with the decisions.

Mothers who are proud of their own achievements at work are excited by the possibility of their daughters seeing them operate outside the home. After reading about Take Our Daughters to Work Day, one mother wrote, "I started a four-year apprenticeship for the Sheet Metal Union in 1984 at the Long Beach Naval Shipyard. I became a sheet-metal mechanic and a union steward. To date, I am still the only female union steward in the production area of the shipyard. If nominated, I plan to run for president of my local. I really love my job and my extra duties and would love sharing a day with my three daughters to help get females exposed to a whole new environment and work experience."

Other mothers took on the responsibility of running the organizing committees that developed the day's activities. And on a day when our nation's mothers shined, so too did many fathers. Many fathers were willing allies in the revolution to unseat sexist thinking and the struggle to combat girls' loss of self-esteem.

A salesman from Honolulu wrote: "As a single father, I am concerned about giving my 7-year-old daughter as many confidence-building experiences as possible. Also, I would like to introduce her to as many career choices as possible in the next two years. I'm sick of the 'sex bomb,' stereotyped women my daughter has to see every day. From the bottom of my heart, I thank you for all you are doing for the self-esteem of little girls everywhere."

Another father wrote: "We arranged for two sessions at our Saturn manufacturing plant here in Tennessee. Since our work force works day and night shifts, we wanted to make sure everyone had an opportunity to bring their daughters to work. Over 80 girls attended, accompanied by their parents. Overall it was a great success. We view this event as a positive step to emphasize diversity efforts within the organization, to support families to do the right things for their children, and to encourage career development for women long-term."

Many girls who participated responded with confidence, enthusiasm, and hope. "When I watch my mom, I feel really good to be a girl," said 12-year-old Christen McLaurin. "I know that I don't have to feel that I'm not as good as the boys or anything."

"I learned that men are not the only ones in high jobs in the world," said another young participant. Kate Martuscello learned that women served as generals in combat and vice presidents and presidents of companies and countries. "All of these women took a stand and were not afraid to speak out about what they thought was right or wrong."

With all the power and possibility the day ignited, there were other realities for parents. In July 1993, the unbearable happened to LuElla Edwards. Her only child, 15-year-old Laquanda, was killed in the cross fire of a gang shootout in front of their home in the Cabrini Green apartment complex in Chicago. Three months earlier, Laquanda had participated in Take Our Daughters to Work Day along with thousands of other Chicago girls. Knowing how much her daughter enjoyed that day, Edwards formed a Take Our Daughters to Work Club as a way of helping other people's daughters stay away from the gang warfare that killed Laquanda. "I thought about my daughter and how much she enjoyed seeing the working world," she said. "I wanted to give other girls that chance." Edwards honored her daughter by providing other girls with a chance to experience opportunities outside their housing project.

Take Our Daughters to Work Day is a challenge to all parents, adults, and boys to respect and support girls as they face the challenges of becoming women. Parents discovered they could inspire change. Now the challenge is to institutionalize it.

Nell Merlino is a communications strategist for the Ms. Foundation for Women. She has also directed a number of highly visible campaigns on issues related to women, health, and the enviroment.

Marian Cleeves Diamond, 67, is a professor of integrated biology and director of the Lawrence Hall of Science at the University of California, Berkeley where she leads a staff of 340. Diamond has also pioneered breakthrough research on the brain. In the photo, Dr. Diamond is standing next to a display on brain synapse, which is part of a permanent exhibition at the Lawrence Hall of Science that attracts more than 300,000 visitors a year.

NO ONE SAID it would be easy, but one needs to remember that it is not only the beginning that counts but the end as well . . . the whole continuum of a lifetime. I proceeded one step at a time over my full 67 years, with at least the next 33 yet to go. Who knows when genetic engineering will allow us to direct our lives in the future?

In my language as a brain scientist I would say we program our "supplementary motor cortex" to help guide our direction. If we are willing to accept the endless challenges as well as risk the unknown with each step, we can somehow fulfill our dreams. No one gave us a blueprint to follow. We have the privilege and the pleasure, each with our unique brains, to plan, execute, and finally accomplish our goals. Dream, for through dreams realities come about.

I have always loved science. When I was 14 I wrote an essay in my English class, "When I grow up, I will attend the University of California at Berkeley because those who don't wish they did."

My fifth and sixth grade grammar school teachers complimented my geometry and English work; my seventh grade teacher showed me the thrill of examining the structure of a fly's wing; in my high school physiology class I loved the synchronous contraction of the chambers in the heart, and in my late teens I saw my first human brain in the Los Angeles County Hospital. The mental picture of that brain is as clear today as it was about 50 years ago. Four doctors in white coats stood around a small square table, in the center of which lay a human brain. I stared with awe because this was a mass that could actually THINK! A writer for *Psychology Today* once wrote, "It was a love affair with a brain."

Upon entering graduate school at the University of California, Berkeley, I not only had the opportunity to study brains, but I earned my way by becoming a teaching assistant for medical students. The first time students asked me a question and I could "teach" them the answer, something special happened inside me. I not only felt good, I felt exhilarated. Had those lazy "teacher genes" found the right environment to express themselves? My Swiss grandmother and mother had both been teachers, but I never imagined that I would feel satisfied in such a role. My English grandfather and doctor father had both been very service oriented. So the combination of teaching and learning about the brain in order to offer something of value to society was a winning combination as far as I was concerned.

People often ask, "What is the most valuable

contribution your research has demonstrated?" I reply with pleasure, "Showing that the cerebral cortex can respond positively to an enriched environment at *any* age." Our little rats placed in either an enriched or impoverished environment have shown that the cerebral cortex (the part of the brain dealing with analytical thinking, judgment, planning, etc.) can either increase its structure with enrichment, or decrease with impoverishment. Such changes occur in the young, the middle-aged, and in the very old. What an optimistic finding to offer society! Now these results have been confirmed in human beings as well, but the rats provided the first guidelines.

Now, after 46 years of teaching, I have had the pleasure of lecturing on every continent but Antarctica. My present human anatomy class at Berkeley has over 700 students. What a pleasure it is to teach these young, eager students—the

health professionals of tomorrow—about "the house in which they will spend their lives," namely their bodies. If only all people could learn about and understand their bodies and how to keep them well. Think of the billions of dollars we could save in health care!

To have the opportunity to be the director of the Lawrence Hall of Science is a great challenge. The staff of 340 serve in our research and development center for science and math education for kindergarden through twelfth grade. Our teacher's guides reach over one quarter of the nation's elementary schools and 32 foreign countries. What a marvelous opportunity to enrich the lives of young minds of every age—to actually use what we have learned in the laboratory. Most of all, I gain a tremendous amount of pleasure from my family, my husband and four children, who have all done very well in their own right—three PhDs and one MD. The quest to create, to learn, and to share goes on and on!

Marva J. Holliday, 57, has been a school crossing guard for 22 years. She also sings and acts, and has been inspired by Billy Holiday, Sarah Vaughan, and Ella Fitzgerald.

I SING JAZZ and blues where and whenever I can. I belong to the Senior Choir and Gospel Chorus of my church, and I'm part of a 50-member choir. A great actress was also a dream of mine, and I am a member of the Drama Guild at my church and perform in numerous productions. My role as Lena Younger in *A Raisin in the Sun* was my finest hour. Now, the question is, what do you do Marva?

I am a school crossing guard for the city of Philadelphia. I am now into my 22nd year and I love my job. My wages are less than $10,000 per year. I work four hours a day, ten months a year. There are no wages or work during July and August, so during the summer months I am a home health aide for a nursing service. I service handicapped and senior citizens in their homes two to four hours a day. This work is very rewarding.

I have not always been a school crossing guard. I also worked as a telephone operator for about 11 years, and a mailroom clerk for about four years, as well as a cab dispatcher, inventory counter, home health aide, clerk-typist, and seamstress. Because I was raising three small children during that time and working at night, I had a babysitting problem and had to resign from the postal service. As you might guess, there was a time period where I worked two jobs. I am qualified to earn $35,000 per year and have been offered a full-time position with the city, starting salary double my present income. Would you believe I turned it down? My friends have said, "You're crazy." But some people have said if you like your job, stay where you are. I love my job.

I love the children and teaching them safety habits in the street. Also, I love the respect from the community and parents as well as from the children. I love the freedom of not being confined indoors, being able to walk to and from work, and all the things I can get done between my working hours.

What I don't like about my job are snowballs. I hate, *hate* snowballs. I don't throw them and I don't like them thrown in my direction. I don't like ice—walking on ice with a constant fear of falling. Also, the arthritis in my legs and hips won't bother me all winter, but when the April rain falls, the good ol' arthritis will pay me a visit causing great pain and discomfort. I have a list of things people do that bother me when I'm working as a crossing guard: red-light runners; non-turn-signal users; tailgaters; red-light crossers; middle-of-the-street crossers; and cross-corners crossers. The last three are done by teenagers and adults and their actions will cause children to copycat.

My benefits with this job are the best part for part-time workers. We all get uniforms, including watches, shoes, boots, handbags, and gloves, along

with a full dental plan, eye glasses, clinic and hospital benefits, legal services, vacation pay, annual leave days, snow days (four per year), funeral days, and sick leave plus eight paid holidays. Yes, I love my job!

Ann Patterson, 47, has been supporting herself for 17 years doing what she loves most, making music. Originally trained in classical music, she is now best known as a jazz musician and the leader of the all-female, 17-member jazz band, Maiden Voyage.

I WORK as a free-lance, professional musician playing many styles of music on various woodwind instruments. On any given day I might be found in a studio orchestra recording a film score, or record album, or in a crowded theater pit juggling several instruments as I accompany the performers on stage. I have led my own 17-piece, all-female jazz band, Maiden Voyage, in a variety of situations, including small jazz clubs, major jazz festivals, the Academy Awards Governors' Ball, and the "Tonight Show." I have jammed with the Posse on the "Arsenio Hall Show," played for the Ice Capades, the Ringling Brothers Circus, the LA Ram's Band, and more weddings and bar mitzvahs than I care to remember.

I don't remember ever not being a musician. As a child I loved to sing. Piano lessons started when I was 7, and I couldn't wait to reach the sixth grade so I could play an instrument in the school band. I wanted to play drums like my dad, but was told it was not a good choice for a girl. I settled for the alto saxophone because we had one at home that my brother had played. In junior high, the band director asked me if I wanted to play the oboe and since it was smaller than the

sax, and easier to carry to school. I said yes.

I grew up in a conservative, small town in west Texas in the 1950s and early '60s—hardly an environment conducive to my becoming who I am today. But I had a wonderful high school band director who encouraged me, as did my college-educated parents who stressed excelling academically as well as musically. My attitude toward picking a profession was shaped by my father who played his way through college and pharmacy school during the Depression. Then it was time to get a "real" job, get married, and raise a family. By the time I knew my father, he was only playing drums a couple of times a year for fun. The summer before my senior year, I attended a National Science Foundation college program for outstanding high school students. My plan was to get interested in something practical like medicine, pharmacy, or psychology, but after eight weeks without music, my decision was easy. My father advised that if I had to go into music, I should prepare myself to teach so I could make a living should the need arise. My plan was to major in performance and teach at a university.

I received a full music scholarship to the University of North Texas. While there, I dated one of the outstanding musicians in its famous jazz department. He introduced me to the music of people like Charlie Parker, Cannonball Adderly, and John Coltrane. I fell in love with jazz. However, learning to play jazz would have to come later since my studies and classical oboe training took up all of my time, and I knew of no women playing jazz. Nobody told me about Melba Liston, who played trombone with and arranged for Dizzy Gillespie, Billie Holiday, and Quincy Jones in the 1940s and '50s. (I didn't find out about her until she and I were both included in the book *American Women In Jazz* published in 1982.) In addition, I still was quite the "Texas girl"—college yearbook beauty, finalist in the Miss Texas Pageant, sorority member—and I just couldn't picture myself as a jazz player.

After earning a master's degree in performance and teaching at a university in Wisconsin, I married, earned another master's degree, this time in music education, and moved to Los Angeles with my husband. It was 1975 and I was teaching elementary music. I had no quality musical outlet. My marriage began to unravel, and for the first time in my life, I really thought about who I was and what I wanted. I knew that playing music—not teaching it—gave me life and happiness in my heart. I didn't know if I could make a living as a musician, but I wanted to try. Inspired by the women's movement, I finally had the confidence to learn to play jazz. The more I studied jazz, the more I knew that it was "home" for me, musically speaking. I loved the freedom of creating the music on the spot—listening to, and interacting with other musicians, first leading and then following. In time, the women's movement freed me as a person, and jazz freed me as a musician.

Many of my first jobs were in female bands where looks outweighed musicianship, and unprofessional treatment and low wages were commonplace. Then in 1979, after swearing that I would never again become involved with an "all-girl band" project unless it paid a whole lot of money,

Photo: Paula Ross

I agreed to help organize a women's big band. I was motivated by the challenge to create a living contradiction to the misconception that female bands were mediocre and unprofessional, and that women were not good jazz players. Little did I know that from this beginning a very special band called Maiden Voyage would emerge. This band has become many things, including a network for women in the music business, a supportive atmosphere in which to develop new skills and gain experience, a showcase to expose talent, a source of income, and an inspiration for aspiring musicians. Maiden Voyage has a reputation for its tight ensemble playing, musicality, and strong soloists. World-renowned jazz critic, Leonard Feather, described the band as "not just the best orchestra of its sex, but one of the most rewarding bands on the present scene."

Although I think of myself simply as a *musician*, I am often reminded that I am a "woman" musician. Sometimes I have gotten work because I am a woman, and sometimes I have lost work because of my sex. I was almost fired from a cruise ship job based on the lame excuse that I would have to share a bathroom with the male musicians. I was able to retain the job only after threatening a law suit. Ironically, I was asked to stay on after I finished the cruise, but I declined. Recently, I was asked to audition for an extensive Bette Midler tour because she wanted a female horn section. When I was offered the job for little more than one-third the salary the male musicians were making, I turned it down.

I have also encountered discrimination within my union. When I filed a job report I had to note the size of the band in a blank labeled "number of men." When a Maiden Voyage jazz quartet played a jazz festival in Arizona, I received a work dues bill from the local union for leader and three "sidemen." In 1985, I ran for the board of directors of the Los Angeles local and was elected, becoming the youngest person on the board, and one of two women. We began changing the sexist language in our by-laws, contracts, etc. Then we submitted a proposition to the American Federation of Musicians national convention to change all sexist language nationwide. I spoke on the proposition while it was being considered by an all-male committee before it was submitted to the convention floor. As I walked in, I was approached by the chairman's assistant, whose first words to me were, "Are you

a wife?" Fortunately, I had support in the room and the proposition passed.

For me, being a musician is about relationships. First, there's the relationship between me and my instruments. I'm glad I didn't get to play the drums because there's something about blowing life into a wind instrument, setting it vibrating with my breath. It's as if the instrument begins deep within my body, connecting my soul to the sound that comes out the bell of the horn. When it's right, the instrument and I are one, and there's nothing else like it for me. Secondly, there's the relationship between me and me. It has never been easy for me to express my feelings verbally. Sometimes in my darkest hours, the only way I am able to get me feelings out is through music. Then there's the relationship between me and the other musicians. I can connect to a total stranger I have nothing in common with when we are on the same musical wavelength. And finally, as I've matured I have developed a relationship between me and my audience. For awhile, I was so self conscious, I had to pretend the audience wasn't there in order to play. Then I began to experience the effect my playing had on people— something I have experienced as a listener. To be able to make a difference in someone else's life— in how they feel—to touch them in a way that they can experience that joy that lies within them—*that* is amazing.

Ann Rodman, 36, works for the National Park Service. She is mapping and sampling the soils of Yellowstone National Park to understand the effects of wildfires that ravaged the park in 1988.

RIGHT NOW I have a great job in one of the most beautiful places on earth. How did I get here? Who knows? It really is a mystery to me how these things work out. My only plan has been to choose interesting places.

I grew up with parents who love the outdoors. They'd rather spend their time and money hiking 20 miles away from a road, or canoeing a wild river, than buying a new car or new clothes. From them I learned to love adventure and wilderness. I've always felt more at home on a mountain than in a building. I used to think everyone grew up that way.

Near the end of high school, I heard about a research project up on the Juneau Ice Field in Alaska. I took a chance and sent in an application. That summer introduced me to geology and field research. I lived on a glacier, measured its movement, and used skis to cross it. This was way too much fun to be a job. At that point I thought working for a living was something I had to do rather than something I'd choose.

Chemistry was my favorite science in high school so I continued with it in college. After a year I found that chemists end up spending their summers, and eventually their lives, in laboratories. This seemed like a terrible waste of summer days. I remembered all those scientists I had met up on the ice field, and I thought that geology might have something going for it. Over the next few years, geology led me to a variety of interesting part-time jobs. I got to dig up dinosaur bones in Montana, map rock outcrops in the Coast Range of British Columbia, Canada, and collect rock samples in the Sinai Peninsula of Egypt. I realized that work could be challenging, interesting, and sometimes, lots of fun. At the end of college I interviewed with big oil companies. The idea of someone paying me lots of money to do geology was hard to ignore. Working in an office didn't sound great, but I still thought that was what real work meant. Then I talked to someone from the Peace Corps, and all thoughts of an air-conditioned office somewhere in Texas vanished.

I ended up in Nepal teaching math and science to grades six through eight. Nepal doesn't have many roads, so I had to walk about four days to find the village I was supposed to live in for the next two years. Quite a challenge when all you know how to do is comment on the weather and ask for rice. I had up to 85 kids in a class, and I spoke the language like a five-year old. You can imagine how entertaining this was for a bunch of seventh graders. Learning a different language had always seemed difficult, if not impossible. Finally, to speak another language was magic for me. It made me pay attention to how people think, and how to get ideas out of my head and into theirs.

For the first time in my life, I was aware of being a minority. I was female in a society where men are officially in charge of everything. Most women in the villages have no formal education. I was white where everyone else was some other color. They thought their color was normal and mine was strange. Growing up white in America hadn't prepared me for that. It was true, I didn't know how to milk a water buffalo or plant rice, or any of the hundreds of other useful things that any ten-year old knows how to do. They wondered how I had survived so long in the world. At first it bothered me when everyone pointed and laughed at me. This kind of openness and honesty was new for me. I mean, I was the one from America who had gotten through Princeton University with honors. This should count for something. Unfortunately, no one in the village had heard of Princeton. So I learned to take myself less seriously and eventually enjoyed laughing at myself almost as much as they enjoyed laughing at me. In an environment where life and death situations are common, you learn not to worry about little stuff. People in the US worry way too much about little things that really aren't that important.

I came back to the States caring as much about who benefited from my work as I did about whether I enjoyed the work. I started studying soils as a way to build on my knowledge of geology and learn about agriculture. I wanted a chance to go back overseas and work in agricultural development. After graduate school, I applied for a four-month job in Yellowstone National Park mapping a small area of soil. This seemed like a great place to get some field experience before I got a real job.

Things went along smoothly for a month or so until the big forest fires. This was obviously an important event, so I quit mapping soils and started on fire research projects. I worked with a team of ecologists and fire specialists. Our plan was to collect data from plots before they burned. We tried to get out early in the morning before the humidity dropped and the fires shot up into the trees. It is amazing how fast you can collect data when trees are burning all around. Sometimes it worked well and sometimes we got chased into the river. The fires focused a lot of attention on the park and its resources. All this interest convinced people that we needed to know more about soils all over the park. Since I was in the right place, I got the job mapping over two million acres of semi-burnt soils.

Basically, I spend the summers outside digging holes and the winters writing about what I find. The work is physically demanding. We carry heavy packs and stay out for up to a week at a time. Sleeping among grizzly bears and bison leaves me a little tense at times, but seeing so many wild animals is a gift I never grow tired of. Everyday I see elk, deer, coyotes, bighorn sheep, bison, moose, and bears. Most of our work is away from the trails. We use compasses and maps to figure out where we are. Some days this works better than others.

The really hard part of my work is back in the office. I sit in front of a computer for days at a time sorting through a confusing pile of information. I try to find patterns that will help me understand how soils form differently under different conditions. This is a hard job anywhere, but I think working in Yellowstone has an added level of difficulty. It seems like everyone in the

Photo: Jeff Henry

country has a different opinion about how the park should be managed. What they all have in common is how passionately they believe that their ideas are the best. It is exciting to be in an environment where everyone cares so much, but it focuses a lot of attention onto every decision we make. There are so many rules and regulations that it sometimes seems hard to move in any direction.

It is good to have dreams and even better to follow them. It helps when other people expect great things from you, but if you are a woman they often don't. This gives you a better chance to surprise everyone. The more things I try, the fewer limits I believe in.

Ramona Ortega, 18, has cooked in various restaurants since she was 15 years old. She also works part time in a specialty produce market and hopes to use her knowledge of the food industry to become a journalist.

Photo: Nita Winter

AS THE DAUGHTER of many generations of women workers, I've grown up with the notion that a lazy person is useless. Consequently work has continually accompanied my life. From the time when my grandmother had us grandchildren doing this and that when we were bored, to working alongside my mother on odd house-cleaning jobs, to my first real paying job: work has always been the key to personal independence and success.

At the fresh age of 15 fate landed me a job in the kitchen of a new cafe. I originally applied to work in the limelight of the espresso bar in hopes of being cool. Instead, I was offered a position assisting the chef during dinner. Graciously accepting the job that paid a lot more than a counter person, I was taken under the wing of a wonderful and experienced person. So there I was, learning the skills and background of classic American and French cuisine, balancing being a cocky teenager by day and a cook by night. The kitchen soon became my niche; a place where the delicate dance between gritty hard work and executing an exquisite meal paid off with every fulfilled diner.

It was an unusual experience to be young and in a profession that warrants admiration. People always say, "Oh, you cook," with a puzzled look. In every kitchen I've worked in, I am always the youngest. Being the youngest is half the fun because I bring a youthful charisma to an already erratic environment. The crew always teases me that I am not old enough to drink the wines that we taste. My age never interfered with me getting hired because they always assumed that I was older. In no way is cooking a glamorous job. You don't know what nice hands are because they usually are recovering from a cut or a burn—and nails, forget it, they are short and dirty. The cooking garb is also attractive; starched white chef's coat always too long for my 5'1" frame, black-and-white checkered pants. And by the end of the night you've acquired such a foul odor from the garlic and raw meats you've touched that you can't stand to smell yourself.

I was lucky I didn't have a soft nerve for the unusually grotesque food preparations. That's the first thing you have to lose, although butchering a rabbit still makes me squirm. One thing I did acquire was a taste for good food. No frozen dinners at my house. Unfortunately, I never seem to maintain the budget for all the gourmet treats I crave. Instead of candy bars, I want baked brie and shiitake mushrooms. Through cooking I earned a decent income and was capable of moving out and living on my own at 16. The kitchen definitely put some years on me.

Although I never had any horrible experiences with sex discrimination, there were times I was the only female on an all-male kitchen staff and there were plenty of subtle reminders that I was female in a male-dominated kitchen. Professional kitchens are contrary to the typical family kitchen where the woman usually has control.

Cooking is an art. The kitchen is filled with artists who concoct masterpieces for the palate. And like an artist, it takes a lot of devotion to become good. Although I enjoy cooking and have made wonderful friends in the business, I definitely do not have the passion needed to remain in this profession.

Recently I decided to leave the restaurant and work for a specialty produce market. The long, late hours and stress on the line can drive anyone to a quick burnout. My professional background in gourmet dining helped me get involved with different aspects of the field. I'm also going to use my experience as a tool to get me into journalism, which is my first love. Having knowledge of the food scene opens up doors to do reviews.

I possess all the traits that typically result in oppression in this business: I'm young, Mexican, and a woman. But I survived and succeeded, and this allowed me the opportunity to work in respected restaurants and learn a skill I can take anywhere, even into my own kitchen where family and friends know they will always enjoy a great meal.

Photo: Nita Winter

RODEO BRONCO RIDER

Marge Dressel, 32, is a bareback bronco rider who works at a rodeo school as well as bartending part time.

BORN AND RAISED on a farm in Northern Minnesota, I've always been physically strong—threw hay bales, broke and trained horses, and worked in the woods for my dad who had a pulp contract with a paper company. My mother was killed by lightning when I was 4 years old, and Dad raised four girls, ages 4 through 10. He taught us to be strong emotionally as well as physically; to go after what we wanted and stand up for what we believed in. I played judo for six years while in high school and took the Minnesota State Tournament as a Brown Belt.

I started barrel racing when I was 19 with my mare that I raised from a baby, and still have after 21 years. We went to many small, amateur rodeos and I was always fascinated by bareback bronco riding. I had mentioned this to my ex-husband, and of course, he would have none of that! Our marriage was a very stormy, abusive and demeaning relationship for me. I was emotionally and physically abused. After nearly ten years, on my 31st birthday, he put me in the hospital and I never went back to him. The counselors and advocates at the battered women shelter brought me back around and helped me rediscover how full and beautiful life can be and how much strength, character and love I really have in me. They made me discover a whole "new me"—

one that was really there all along. I vowed to myself that no one and nothing, no matter how rough things get, will ever bring me down again. I depend on myself and go for it in everything I do and in every part of my life. My new philosophy is, "Every day's a holiday and every meal's a feast!"

I was ready for a change and had the opportunity to move to New Mexico. So, I packed up everything I owned, loaded my horses, and headed south. I began training on a mechanical bull at a rodeo school, and a week later I got on my first horse. According to the owner, no woman had ever tried bronco riding at his school, but he figured his horses "were equal opportunity buckers—they will buck anybody off." I made the eight-second ride, but not knowing enough to hang on until the pick-up rider got to me, I

Photo: Alexandria King

48

Photo: Alexandria King

fell off and busted three ribs. I rode the following seven weeks with my ribs wrapped, although the doctor said I couldn't ride at all. Painful! But I was hooked after the first ride and nothing was going to stop me. I've been riding one or two horses a week ever since.

My friends and coaches at the rodeo school have helped back me all the way. Of course, I've encountered opposition in a couple of different instances. There are those who figure I'm out there to attract attention or see what I can find to sleep with—not true at all! I'm there to prove nothing to anyone but myself. There've been rumors started about me and two different cowboys have actually left because women are riding at the rodeo school. My pick-up partner, also a

gal, and I have met up with scorn, ridicule and resistance to our being the ones out there, responsible for getting the cowboys off safely after their ride. But we've shown them we do a good job, and we work well together as a team. We've had to work hard to gain their respect, but now most of them are behind us all the way.

Riding bareback horses has become a driving force in my life. I want to be the best and I'm working hard. It's an almost indescribable high feeling! It's like being on a stick of dynamite, not knowing which way it's going to explode—twisting, turning, tossing you up and slamming you down. It's the longest, most exciting eight seconds of my life. I don't know anyone who has more fun than me!

Mai Wah Ting, 49, is a medical doctor based in Santa Fe, New Mexico. Dr. Ting is in private, family practice. She says she is "just another woman at work."

FROM THE TIME I was a little girl I always knew I was going to be a doctor. There was a sister, before I was born in China, who became very sick with diphtheria because during World War II in China there was no immunization program available. My sister, Jen Jen, became terribly ill and could not breathe.

My parents took her to the hospital, but the doctor refused to do the tracheotomy until he was paid. It was Saturday night, and my father rushed around the town borrowing money from friends. When he returned to the hospital, my sister was dead, laying in my mother's arms. My parents decided to have another child and that child was me. This has been a great burden to me, and also an inspiration. Now, after many years of being a doctor, I accept the road which fate has set for me. I firmly believe that all people deserve access to medical care regardless of ability to pay. Health is a prerequisite to the pursuit of happiness.

After I finished medical school, internship, and residency, I was personally disillusioned with the practice of medicine in this country. This was in the late 1960s when so many of us were disillusioned by the American way of life. I chose in the face of war, a quest to find inner peace. That quest took me to a remote rural valley in the mountains of southeast Colorado. I learned to love that beautiful, desolate valley. Facing a minus 40-degree temperature in a raging blizzard was easier for me to deal with than a drunkard's hurtful outburst, "Hey, China girl—when I was in Shanghai during the war …"

There were other people who were drawn to the valley during those years in search of alternatives. As we built our families and our homes, it became obvious that the community needed health care services. People came to me for help and advice. After a particularly bitter experience trying to help parents find medical care for their sick baby who was bleeding internally, I decided to get my medical license to practice. It wasn't an easy decision. I like my privacy; I like my freedom. I knew my family's life would be disrupted.

There's too much paranoia surrounding a doctor practicing medicine in the United States. Malpractice looms above our heads. Americans are too busy buying things with a 50,000 mile-warranty. They want Life translated into a guarantee. And how does a doctor guarantee you a perfect baby, a perfect operation, a perfect cure? I knew for years I wanted nothing to do with obtaining malpractice insurance. To me medical care was an agreement between the doctor and the patient—a bond of trust between two people. I thought that if I tried my best and taught the patient to accept responsibility for his or her own health, I could avoid a malpractice suit. If I can't operate on this principle, it just doesn't make sense to me even to practice medicine. Well, I ate

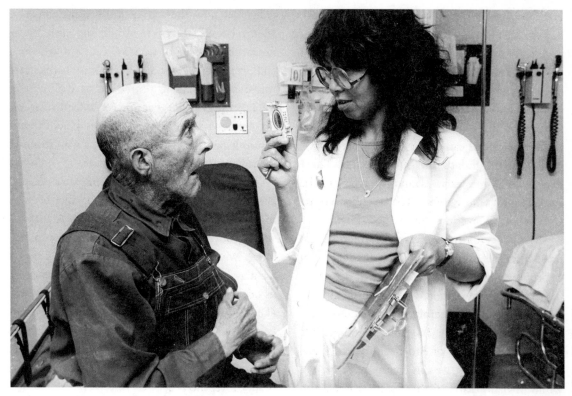

my words. I now have malpractice insurance.

People say doctors make a lot of money— remuneration for our time. I haven't found that to be true, especially if you're taking care of poor people. Most of my patients have tried to pay me something, but there are those who justify in their minds that the time I spent wasn't really worth it. It was more important to buy a car, a satellite dish, or a six-pack of beer. And I guess those are the ones I remember when I'm feeling "burnt out" and "used." But there are also those really special moments when there is a smile, like when a baby is born, that makes it all worth while.

I moved to Santa Fe to work at the peniten-

tiary of New Mexico. It's a hard-core prison as far as prisons go, but I took the job because I just wanted a job, and it afforded me the time to spend with my children. Having a 9-to-5 job made it possible for us to have a more regularly scheduled life. I remember, back in Gardner, Colorado, my daughter, Shamai, wrote me a note saying how much she loved me, but how come we only ever ate in the dark. Being a single mother and a rural doctor stretched all our resources as a family.

I also worked with Women's Health Sources in Santa Fe, which was started as a cooperative in the wake of the women's movement. It serves the poor people in Santa Fe. I was fired from my job after seven years. I was shocked. However, it liberated my mind to accept finally that I can work as a doctor for money as well as for service, that I personally am not responsible for the greed of doctors who only do it for money (such as the one who refused treatment to my dying sister in China so many years ago). Most important, I have learned to value myself as a unique individual rather than what I can do for others in service; be it my children, friends, lovers, or patients. This I share with all my sisters around the world in the awakening of who we are. This has enhanced my abilities and compassion to be a good doctor.

My two children are grown and ready to meet the challenges of the world. Presently, I'm in private, family practice. My focus in doctoring has to do with prevention. I work with people in altering lifestyles to maximize physical, emotional, and spiritual well-being. I see this as a direct side effect of the affluence of American society. Here, in the United States, we can choose what we eat, while in many parts of the world women and their children are starving. Sometimes I wonder at the absurdity of the American obsession with dieting and appearing "attractively slim." We have so many obese people, who despite their caloric intake, are not ingesting adequate vitamins, minerals, amino acids (protein), and carbohydrates to maintain health. I see the pathos that is in all of us Americans: The act of eating is more than just that—it's a way of feeling loved and nurtured.

I am deeply concerned about the degradation of our environment; how our factories and automobiles are polluting our air and water. The soil is being leached of its minerals by fertilizers and pesticides. The native people of the Southwest used to sustain themselves on a diet of beans, corn, and chile, but now they suffer from iron-deficiency anemia because there is no iron in the earth. So, in my work I talk about what we eat, how we work and play, how we rest and sleep. I use herbs, vitamins, homeopathic remedies, as well as the miracle drugs. I advocate prayer and meditation. Sometimes I just listen. Sometimes I hold them. I'm so lucky (finally) that I am not a man so that I can't be accused of sexual harassment.

Touching my patients in a loving way, not just clinically, took a long time to get together because of the professional training I received. Actually, I started out by massaging them. Stress is a big thing. We are all stressed out to the *max*. I try to see it as positive. Stress isn't some monster inside of us or some horrible thing that is happening to us, like a mean boss, lousy hours, or a bad marriage. It's how we view it. Yet, I also see how stress manifests as disease. I believe that within each and everyone of us is the power to heal; to manifest beauty, love, and peace.

Marian Wright Edelman, 55, is founder and president of the Children's Defense Fund. CDF works to educate the nation about the needs of children. Edelman attended Yale Law School and was the first black woman to be admitted to the Mississippi bar. She serves on the board of the NAACP Legal Defense and Education Fund, the March of Dimes Birth Defects Foundation, and the Robin Hood Foundation.

AS A PARENT, I always wanted to make sure my three sons had all the opportunities and "things" I didn't have while growing up. I also wanted to shield them from the problems and barriers I faced and overcame as a black child and a black woman.

But as a parent, I could not ignore other people's children or their pain. This pain spills over into the public space and threatens the safety and quality of life and the future of my own sons. Loving my sons means struggling every day for a lifetime to give them and all children a better world than the one I inherited.

I have often felt the conflict and guilt of rushing off to work to help all children rather than being with my own. Yet I have been fortunate to have real choices. As my own boss, I could skip a meeting to tend to an ear infection or watch a son play baseball. And I had the partnership of a husband and "Miz Amie," who lived with us for 13 years, in raising my sons. It pains me to think of all the mothers who love their children as I love mine but whose choices are far harder than

mine: to buy food or pay rent; to leave a sick child home alone or risk being fired for missing work; to pay the heating bill or buy medicine for my child.

I hope and pray I can help more parents recognize that being parents is the most important calling we have, and that we share a responsibility toward every child in our nation. What we teach children through what we do, what we say, and how we act every day shapes the future of America more than any other effort of our lives.

Photo: Nita Winter

DRY CLEANERS WORKER

Therese Martin Cain, 20, works part time at a dry cleaners as a trainee on the Community Independent Training for Youth Program. Born a Down's syndrome child, and the youngest of seven children, she has been raised with much the same experiences as her five older sisters and older brother, including family vacations, a trip to Europe, and skiing in winter. She graduated from high school as a Special Education student. Cain dictated the following statement about her work to her mother.

I WORK AT the cleaners and live with my family. Working in the back of a cleaners is like working in a jungle. I hang clothes by tags, different color tags. Blue is Monday. Red's for Tuesday. Pink's for Wednesday. Orange is for Thursday. Yellow's for Friday. White's for Saturday. I like best to do paper hangers. It's the easiest. I just put the hangers through the paper. I am pretty fast. Sometimes you see spots, then I get Mike (supervisor) to work on the spots.

I like the people where I work. I do like Mike, but there's one thing about him—he's like a good friend. He understands how I feel. Others make nice comments about me like "Terry's great." They know I'm a good worker and I know they like the way I do my work.

Some things I don't like are getting confused when things don't go just right and when I don't know where to put things when I don't understand. I don't like problems, but I don't seem to be having any now. Sometimes I get tense with Mike when he corrects me.

I'm glad I have the job. It makes me feel good and I like the way people treat me. My boss makes jokes: "Here's your paycheck; go out and get drunk." That was his joke. The ladies who work at the desk up in front are sometimes funny and they are very nice. I think they like to reach out to me, and I like the way they treat me. I think my job is great, though sometimes I get the ups and downs—mad, sad, or hurt. If I do, I have to solve the problem.

Photo: Gary McCarthy

Sheba W. Naquin, 30, teaches third and fifth graders in the classroom as well as in a computer lab.

WHEN I FIRST got out of high school, I just knew I wanted to do clerical work—typing, filing, etc. I also liked writing essays in high school.

I worked for the federal government at the Social Security building in Richmond for a while, working as a records analysis clerk and clerk-typist. I could type 75 words a minute. It was very nice doing that kind of work, but as the years passed, my mind began to change.

I have always wanted to have children but have had a very rough time. I've had six miscarriages. I just wanted to be with kids and help other people with their kids, so I decided to go into child care. I went through nine months of training in a child care program and after a couple of months, I got a job with a YWCA child care center. After working there a year, I got pregnant again and needed bed rest, so I had to quit my job. But that pregnancy ended in a miscarriage, too.

In 1986, I took a written test to work for the school district and I passed. I like working for the school district because I get lots of vacation time at Christmas, spring break, and during the summer. I get paid about $8 an hour. Working with kids is rewarding, but it isn't always easy. There's a lot of stress. I teach third and fifth graders who come from a ghetto neighborhood where there are a lot of drugs and such. We haven't had prob-lems with drugs and violence in school, but sometimes the kids yell at you or come in with a bad attitude, which makes them hard to teach. Some kids try to disrupt the classroom and have to be sent to the principal's office.

I work at two local elementary schools, one in the morning and the other in the afternoon. I teach children in the classroom as well as in the computer lab. I get to do a little clerical work also. I like working with computers mostly because of the typing. I really love to type.

I'd still like to have a family but I don't think about it much. I have lots of nieces and nephews, so my sisters tell me that I already have a lot of kids. And I feel I'm giving something of myself to all the kids in school.

Photo: Nita Winter

IRON WORKER

Patsy L. Davis, 38, is an iron worker who hopes that when her granddaughter grows up, women on a construction job will be just old hat.

FOR MY SIZE, at 5'1 ½" tall and about 110 pounds, I am a rather petite-looking grandmother who is also an apprentice iron worker. The work is heavy and hard on the body. It sure builds up muscles and I will have some pretty good muscles if I live through this program that lasts three years. I am still in my first year, but I've got to make it since I can't type!

An iron worker is a construction worker who puts up the iron, decking, steel stairs, handrails, and the all-around structural steel in bridges, hotels, high rises, whatever. We do about all the fabrication of the metal that goes into a building and almost all of the welding that holds the place together. As an iron worker, I have to be able to read many types of blueprints. We also put together the big cranes that do the heavy lifting on construction sites along with the rigging; moving large equipment in and around a building; and setting the steel that is the backbone of any large building. It's not unusual to be working 20 stories up on a building that will top out at 32 floors.

I've always wanted to travel and construction workers do travel with the job. Before now I never had the chance to reach out into fields that may include travel because I was raising my children. Now with one married and the other living with his father, I can reach out. I got the chance to get into an iron workers' program and took it. I get paid while I learn on the job. I'm rather old for an apprentice and this does cause problems with the attitude of some I have to work with. My size and sex also cause some of the men to expect me not to be able to do my part. Their attitude does cause me anxiety at times, but on the whole, I've found that most of the men will give a woman a chance if she shows she really wants to learn and do her work.

I feel a woman has the right to earn a good wage as much as a man. She really has to work for the chance in construction. You have to give it your all. The work is heavy. The weather is either hot or cold and the hours can be very long. The strong language used by the men has to be overlooked. After all, most of these guys have been at this work for years and have always talked like that, and just because a woman wants to try the work doesn't give her the right to dictate how a man talks. As long as the words are not aimed at me, I just shut them out.

The work can be very hard and I pray that I have the willpower to hold on till I can become a really good iron worker. By the time my grandchild grows up, I hope that women on a construction job will be just old hat. After all, she may very well want to be one of the iron workers one day.

Photo: Kathleen Smith–Barry

ARCHITECT

Elizabeth Ericson, 54, has been an architect for the past 24 years. She is the first woman to be promoted to partner at the Boston firm of Shepley, Bulfinch, Richardson, and Abbott, the oldest firm in the country.

BECOMING AN ARCHITECT takes a long time. After 28 years in the business, four years of architectural school, and four years of liberal arts education, I am still learning. At 17, I was all set to be a journalist, then I went to the Yucatan and saw the ancient Mayan city, Chichen Itza. Limestone structures gleamed in the jungle, their geometries crisp and beautiful. Silent cities spoke to me of the human spirit, which once inhabited them. I was moved. I decided to study architecture.

I graduated from Columbia School of Architecture in 1966 after four intensive years of engineering, construction, painting, sculpture, history, and principles of design. Living in New York City was an architectural textbook all by itself. After school, I traveled around the world on a fellowship to see the buildings I had only read about. I sketched them. I was elated. But I needed to learn more to become useful to the practice, so I got a job as an office apprentice, and for very little pay. At my first job as a designer-draftsman my lettering was wiggly. I was told that I would be fired unless the letters were straighter and more consistent. Being an architect can be a humbling experience sometimes, especially after all that education.

In 1972, I took the four-day state test, and was licensed to practice architecture under my own name. I had to decide whether or not to stay in the firm I worked in or start my own practice. I decided to start a small office with my architect husband and two employees to design residential buildings. I spent a lot of time in administration, client and employee relations, but not enough time on designing and building. I am now a partner at the Boston firm of Shepley, Bulfinch, Richardson and Abbott. It's the oldest firm in the country with a very young spirit. I am the first woman in the firm in that position. There are 175 employees.

The specific issues I face as a woman in architecture are the same issues that anyone faces in the profession, namely, credibility. What does a woman, especially a woman designer, know about technical things? I overcame this doubt by working extensively in the field supervising construction. My knowledge was firsthand, and better than most architects who stayed behind their office desks and drafting tables. To my delight, management issues are shared by all the partners so that there is time for design.

As an architect, I have chosen to humanize and beautify the most technical and sterile of buildings: hospitals. I see no reason why these very important medical "city states" are any different from those Mayan cities I visited. I like to bring daylight and gardens into medical treatment spaces, and to create vistas and axes to dignify the human spirit, as well as nooks and crannies to offer comfort. I have completed six major hospitals, and they are little by little achieving these goals.

What do I do, specifically? I can be inspecting granite samples at a fabricating plant, presenting design ideas to a client, and discussing the progress of a job with the team, all in a day. No day is the same; no year is the same either. The computer revolution has taken hold, and almost 50 percent of the staff are computer literate. The entire profession is learning new skills. Ours is a lifetime of learning, to survive and to remain vital and relevant.

Aspiring to do my personal best includes being a partner of a large firm. I have noticed that we women often remain silent about our objectives and our accomplishments, assuming someone will notice our good work, and promote us. This seldom happens. Communicating to others about what is important to me has helped immeasurably in discovering and creating a pathway for my personal growth and promotion.

The most frustrating aspect of the practice of architecture is that there are so many people involved. Decisions are not simply made. They evolve from meetings, reviews, and budget cuts. The challenge is to emerge with the idea you had in the beginning, improved, shining, and polished. The rewards? That one's imagination can become reality. That the imaginative use of space and light can bring dignity and hope into our lives. That one can achieve beauty.

Photo: Marjorie Nichols

Emma C. Chappell, 51, is the founder and CEO of United Bank, the first black-controlled, full-service commercial bank chartered in Pennsylvania since 1921. Her first bank job was as a clerk/photographer at $45 a week. Since then, Chappell has received numerous accolades, awards, and appointments for her social and political endeavors, as well as three honorary doctoral degrees.

"THIS IS a man's world," and oh, how true it seems! During my growing years, as far back as I can remember, I was faced with male chauvinism as well as a society that was immersed in hatred, malice, and prejudices—from racism to the question of what side of the street you lived. Added to these most disturbing features of the society I had to grow up in—without choice—I also was preoccupied with the economics of life. Finding the means to educate and prepare myself properly for coping with the ups and downs of life was not *anything* close to having it "handed to me on a silver platter."

Of course, like most women, I dreamed of having a family—a husband and children. But ever since I was young, I was obsessed with wanting to be *somebody*. My ambitions were to strive to be in a position where I could help others, to be of service to "my people," to make a contribution to society in general, and have an impact on the lives of the young and the old alike. I must admit that while it is true that I detested discrimination and prejudices of any sort, it is perhaps these very evils that challenged me more and created a motivational charge for achieving success.

Many times as a career woman I have been discouraged and disappointed by the distorted perception of the so-called "man's world" that relegated women to the artificial glass ceiling of professional upward mobility. "A woman's place is in the home," is another common saying that was used when the all-so-domineering male wants to push women aside for want of a better way of dealing with a situation that involves a female counterpart. I think it is referred to as the "male ego." In addition to the sexism, I have also been very aware of the limits to upward mobility based on racism.

My approach to overcoming these hurdles was first to develop a sense of direction, purpose, and discipline. In order not to lose these invaluable attributes, I decided that I would seize every opportunity to improve myself academically and career wise, but never forgetting to put the good Lord first. Educationally, I can say that acquiring several degrees was not smooth and easy, but a disciplined mind, hard work, and a sense of purpose saw me through. I received a bachelor's and a master's both in business and banking, as well as three honorary doctoral degrees in Law, Civil Law, and Humane Letters.

I started my career in banking as a clerk/photographer at $45 a week. I later became vice president of Continental Bank in Philadelphia, thus becoming the first woman vice president of a major commercial bank in Pennsylvania. Now, I am founder, chairman, and chief executive officer of United Bank of Philadelphia, which is truly a "dream come true." United Bank is the first black-controlled, full-service commercial bank chartered in Pennsylvania since 1923. By creating this bank I have realized my vision of making a contribution to "my people." Because of the many sad and unhealthy experiences of growing up with discrimination, poverty, and crime that plagued the neighborhoods, I made a vow that I would do something for the underprivileged, underserved, and minorities. United Bank is the vehicle through which capital can be mobilized for reinvestment in the infrastructure of the cities, neighborhoods, businesses, and people.

As for my family life, I can say with pride that I have two beautiful daughters, Tracey and Verdaynea, and one sweet grandson, Troy, who brings me great joy. Both of my daughters are professionally qualified in business administration and nursing. They are also both happily married.

I am very grateful to my dear loving parents for bringing me up in a Christian home. And as I reflect on my past, I find great consolation knowing that it is because of His grace that I have reached this far. My achievements in my life have always been undergirded by a strong faith in God.

I think that I can safely say I have achieved most of what I set out to achieve in my formative years. I wanted to make a contribution to society—I have done that. I trust that I have made an impact for positive change in some communities. I wanted to help my people and prove that women have the ability and competence to achieve as much as any man, if not more. I have done that. I have sought to be disciplined, purposeful, and God fearing. I pray that I remain committed to those moral ideals, which I believe are valuable in creating a stable, just, and honest world. Let's pray that we can all make a difference.

Mali Sastri, 17, writes and performs her own music in coffee houses.

I THRIVE ON hard work. The very thought of laboring, toiling, struggling, of sweat dripping down the forehead, of exhaustion in the brain or the muscle, excites me. Even the words we use to express hard work—effort, exertion, strain—have a ring to them I find irresistible.

I have always been somewhat like this. Even as a child my favorite game to play with my friends, at recess and at home, was one in which we were characters who worked in a shopping mall. My character lived in her store.

Now that I'm 17 I still need to immerse myself completely in whatever I'm doing. Nowadays it's usually music. I love the work I do for my music: the writing, the playing, the practicing. Music has taught me much more about hard work and its payoff then any after-school job ever could. I've truly learned, from my own, precious experience that, with hard work, dreams can come true.

I've dreamed of being a rock singer ever since I first heard Cyndi Lauper belt out her few notes in "We are the World," when I was in second grade. At that time, music was already a part of my life. In fact, I learned to talk by singing "Mary Had a Little Lamb." I started taking piano lessons, after years of elaborating "Heart & Soul" on my own, when I was 8. I made up my first songs when I was 12.

It's hard to draw the line between natural talent and hard work. My piano teacher always has raved about my "good ear," but she also thought I needed glasses because I didn't practice. And sure, I had the dream of singing with a strength and power that would leave an audience baffled. When it came down to it, though, my singing voice was weak and I despised it. But I had a dream, a destination, and I was ready to work towards it.

The cringing I did when I first listened to my voice on tape, and the envy I had for other singers who could do what I wanted to do, all melt away when I perform at a coffee house's open mike and hear the applause and "encore!" I'm told that it's usually for "great vocals." Just to play at a coffee house is an achievement. It took not only hours of rehearsing, but hours of making phone calls, checking around, getting rides into and out of the city, spending Saturday nights in the basement of a church, and listening to open mikers who make even the most easy-going audience embarrassed and uncomfortable. All the hard work seems worth it. All the struggles and headaches over sight-reading, the hours of pounding fingers into the keys until they memorize their moves is insignificant at the recital when my playing brings tears to an audience member's eyes. That's when I can say yes, it was worth it.

Sometimes, too, it's the work itself that is most satisfying. I love spending hours up in my room in my mini-studio, arranging my songs on the synthesizer. In fact, if it doesn't take me a sizable amount of time and toil to finish a song, I feel that something is missing, something isn't right,

Photo: Rynne

and I won't ever really feel bonded with that song.

Most often, it is the combination of effort and result that keeps me working. When the writing, arranging, singing, and recording are all done and I pop the finished tape into my cassette player, turn the volume up, press play, and flop down on my bed, exhausted, that's when I remember why I love music, and why I could never do anything else.

People say to me, "Oh, the life of a musician is so hard!" But I want to sweat and strain and struggle. I want to pay my dues. I believe that the thought of living where you work, as in the game of my childhood, should not be a frightfully unpleasant thought. To love one's work is to be happy, and it depresses me to see people who dread their daily jobs.

As one who has the tendency to work hard, I often have to step back and say whoa, slow down, relax. You're not getting enough sleep, you're putting too much pressure on yourself. I know plenty of stories of people, artists especially, whose work literally killed them. I'm still learning to find the balance between work and play, but as I see it, there's not much difference between the two. I see work as a synonym for life, a journey that is sometimes most meaningful in its times of blood, sweat, and tears.

MAVIS GRUVER

In 1993, the parents of twin adolescent daughters living in Duluth, Minnesota launched an unusual and refreshing magazine for girls. New Moon: The Magazine For Girls and Their Dreams *is produced through a collaborative process involving girls and adults. The magazine is edited and written by girls, ages 8 to 14, and guided by a 25-member, all-girl editorial board. The publishers and editorial board were honored as "Feminists of the Year" by the Feminist Majority Foundation for their work to promote women's equality in 1993. Mavis Gruver, the daughter of publishers Nancy Gruver and Joe Kelly, writes about her experiences with the magazine and the importance of girls communicating with one another.*

HI, MY NAME is Mavis Gruver. I'm on the editorial board of *New Moon: The Magazine for Girls and Their Dreams*. It may seem strange that I'm editing a magazine, even though I'm only 13. But I like it and I'm good at it. I love reading stories, poems, and articles sent in by girls. I have fun making decisions and knowing that what I say counts. I also like to share my ideas and have discussions about editing *New Moon*.

There are about 25 girls on *New Moon's* editorial board. We meet twice a month for a few hours and go through submissions, decide what future magazines will be about, and do other work. We don't have too many disagreements because we know what's good and what isn't. We get mail from people all over the world. Once we got a letter and painting from a girl in Ukraine.

We used her painting on the cover of one of our issues and had her write her life story inside.

My experience with *New Moon* has been interesting. I have been quoted and interviewed in newspapers and magazines all over the country. I was also on "Good Morning America" and kids' news shows on Nickelodeon TV talking about *New Moon*. I went to New York City for "Good Morning America" and it was cool. It feels really good to see what you've worked on for so long finally printed and out to subscribers and stores. I really like to hear people's input because it helps us improve and refine what we're doing.

My mother came up with the idea of starting a magazine for girls and their dreams in 1992. She started the magazine because my twin sister and I were approaching adolescence and she didn't want us to lose our voices the way many girls do. A lot of the time girls are told that the most important thing is to be pretty and nice.

A Minneapolis girl wrote to *New Moon* and said, "Please listen. I just need someone to talk to. They call me fat. I know I'm not but I suck (my stomach) in anyway. They put me down and then laugh at my try at self-defense. The worst thing about it is that they're my friends."

An Illinois girl wrote to tell how hard it was for her to be 13. She says she thinks she's too tall, too skinny, and a klutz. "People talk about growing like it's a good thing. They even go so far as to call it blossoming. I don't call it blossoming. I call it shrinking; shrinking into somebody who wishes she could go someplace and hide until

she's the perfect size and shape."

These are feelings a lot of girls have. But at *New Moon*, we think girls should feel strong and good about themselves no matter how they look. Growing up should be a good thing for a girl, not something that makes her feel like shrinking and hiding.

After my mother came up with the idea, a group of girls got together to plan what the magazine would have and we started working on it. Some of the things each issue includes are a profile of a girl in a different country and her customs, letters, poems, stories, and drawings from girls around the world; profiles of accomplishments that girls and women have made; cartoons and jokes; science and math projects, and herstory.

New Moon is centered around helping girls communicate with one another. My friend, and co-editor, Elizabeth Sproat, describes the magazine as a "giant telephone wire that connects girls all over the world." The girls who write us know that they can say whatever they want to say in *New Moon* and that's what we want.

Probably the most popular section in the magazine is one called "How Aggravating." Lots of girls write to it and lots of adults focus on it when they read or write about *New Moon*. "How Aggravating" describes inequities that girls experience in everyday life. For example: When you graduate from college, why do you get a *bachelor's* degree?

One day our teacher said something that really

made me mad! He said, "To relieve stress you can play basketball or football, and you girls can watch TV."

Why does Game Boy have "boy" in it? Don't they think girls are cool enough to play it? It should be called Game Kid, or something.

There are both boys and girls on my soccer team. But on our soccer uniform shirt, there is a picture of a boy kicking a ball. Plus lots of times other teams say playing us is going to be easy because there are girls on the team. That's not fair.

When my teacher wants a window opened, she says, "Muscles on the windows, guys!" Then it takes two or three boys to open a window that one girl can open. I hate when she does that.

At *New Moon*, we just don't focus on the bad things, though. We always have articles about girls doing fun, exciting, and important things. Once we wrote about a group of girls who started their own support group at a Florida public housing project to fight drugs, violence, and stereotypes about African-American girls. We interviewed an 11-year-old girl who flew a private plane solo across the country. We profiled a girl professional rodeo rider, a girl training a puppy to be a canine companion for a person in a wheelchair, a girl who started an international kids environmental group, and a girl from a poor New York neighborhood who wrote and published her diary.

New Moon is the way it is because we want it to be real girls connecting with real girls. Girls have written to us about their lives, their experiences, their views, their dreams, concerns, and feelings. *New Moon* is different than other girls' magazines because it is edited by girls and it doesn't have articles about makeup, boys, or fashions. Girls who write us sometimes mention these things, but they seem a lot more interested in other things. Girls have a lot of interests and concerns, but adults (and most girls' magazines) don't give them credit for those ideas.

Not everything about *New Moon* is wonderful, for me at least. My parents both work on it full time and constantly talk about "the magazine this, and *New Moon* that" day and night. As much as I like it, it does get kind of annoying at times. The magazine is run out of the attic in my home, which adds to my aggravation as well. For example, when I'm home from school sick, strangers are coming and going and the phones are always ringing.

Sometimes reporters want to interview me because my mother started the magazine, even when I don't feel like talking to them. Probably the most annoying question they ask is, "What do you want to be when you grow up? A writer or publisher?" I don't know what I want to be when I grow up, and since I'm only 13, I shouldn't have to know. As much as I like working on *New Moon*, I'm quite sure I don't want to be in publishing when I grow up.

All in all, I've had a really great experience with *New Moon*. The editing is fun, but sometimes it's hard to pick between one great article or another. I love to hear other girl's opinions about their lives and the lives of others in the world. I would say to other girls to pursue their dreams and make their wishes come true.

This is a poem that my neighbor, friend and co-editor Amanda Sarette wrote about the magazine.

New Moon is a girl's voice
Floating out on a silent night
Telling her dreams to whom
Will listen
New Moon is girl's spirit
Soaring on the night's shore
Paying attention to her dream
Not someone telling her how to act
Or feel
Let the New Moon Girl Fly

Photo: Sherry Boyce

Rosa Torres, 35, is one of 30 women firefighters in a force of 3,000 employed by the city of Los Angeles. She was recently promoted to engineer, a job which entails driving and maintaining the fire engine.

"**OH,** you work for the fire department? You must be a paramedic…no? Then you do administrative work, don't you?"

It's quite entertaining to see just how incredulous some people are at the thought of female firefighters. But on the other end of the spectrum are those (few) who are proud at what I have accomplished. I've been working as a firefighter for over ten years now and I wouldn't trade it for the world.

Being a firefighter has not been easy, nor do I ever expect it to be. I was actively involved in most of the major fires in LA (the library fire, high-rise fires, etc.), the LA riots in 1992, the "fire storm" brush fires of 1993, and the earthquake fires, explosions, and life rescues of 1994, and yet I am continuously proving myself. Those I've not yet worked alongside are hard pressed to give affirmation to my credibility, but some who have been on the front lines with me are my most ardent supporters. Still, I cannot think of anything more rewarding or fulfilling. I held a wide variety of positions prior to joining the department—everything from private secretary to telephone installer to dancer—nothing compares with being a firefighter.

It's more emotionally demanding than many other types of employment, but the guys here empathize. We all know what it's like to have to go into a burning building and step over dead bodies in hopes of reaching those who may be alive. No one else can understand that. You come to know your co-workers very well, and your lives depend on each other. While everyone else is running out of a burning building, we are running in! My adrenalin starts pumping, my heart rate increases, and my body knows that it's time to go to work. This job demands that your body perform well beyond the limits your mind has set for it. The well-being of lives and the preservation of property are at stake and it's up to me and my co-workers to protect them.

Three years ago I was promoted to engineer. My responsibilities include maintaining the fire engine (oil change, minor mechanical and electrical repairs, lube), trouble shooting its functional problems, safely transporting the crew to emergencies (with red lights and siren!) and making the necessary hose hookups and split-second mathematical calculations to ensure the most effective settings and pressures for firefighting.

By maintaining and operating the fire engine I have come to know its capabilities and limitations. This knowledge is of extreme importance since I drive on the wrong side of the street, run red lights, and swerve around stopped traffic, all at high speeds. I love it! There can be no hesitation in decision making or timing. It's exciting, gripping, challenging, and gratifying, to name a few.

Photo: Theodora Litsios

I receive quite a few doubletakes from the other drivers on the road and even an occasional thumbs-up. I felt drawn to this position. Perhaps it's because I have four sisters, no brothers, a mother who stands by her daughters' decisions and a father that wanted us to be self-sufficient. (Prior to allowing us to obtain a driver's license we had to be capable of reading a map, changing the oil, and changing a tire.)

If my fire company is part of the first-alarm assignment I perform my engineering tasks. But if we're dispatched later on into the incident, I primarily fight fire. After a job well done, there are pats on the back, handshakes, and joviality all around. But when lives are lost, it's taken personally and gloom hangs in the air. Those most deeply affected can always find a sympathetic ear and compassionate understanding to help them through it. Our lives depend on each other which builds a very strong bond. I'm the only female on my shift of 14 members and I feel I've gained 13 brothers. I know I can depend on them to do their jobs and back me up and they have reciprocal respect for me.

Amanda Bergson-Shilcock, 17, has been working since she was 7 years old. She is a writer, a library aide, and a student.

WHEN I WORK, what I do is not always what the world traditionally classifies as work. But that's no surprise in some ways. My whole life has been non-traditional. I've been entirely home schooled (I use this term because it is the most common one; I prefer to define my educational experience as self-directed). I'm now 17, and throughout my life I've had many opportunities to do real work.

From the ages of 7 to 10, I ran several home-based businesses, including a bakery. I sold hundreds of cookies and muffins to family and friends. One of the things I cherished most about this experience was the freedom I had—to make my own mistakes and learn from them, to take on my own responsibilities.

If I accepted an order on Friday afternoon for eight dozen cookies by Saturday morning, it was my responsibility to get those cookies made and delivered. My customers weren't interested in hearing why I couldn't do it—they just wanted their cookies. When I went to the grocery store to buy supplies, it was my job to find the best values. Nobody was standing in line behind me, ready to bail me out if I overspent. I had a wonderful time.

During that same period, I wrote, edited, and published a newspaper called the *Dolltown Daily News*, and sold it (for one cent a copy) to the dolls that inhabited the region of our house known as Dolltown. I also wrote short fiction for my own enjoyment.

I think it was my family's casual yet certain acceptance of the fact that I was working when I was writing that pushed me to view my writing in the same way. My parents showed respect for what I was doing and never seemed to see my work as "kid's stuff." I was always taken seriously, and I have fond memories of reading my very first short story out loud at the dinner table. That story is buried in a deep pile of things I'd rather forget now, but it started me off on a long path of writing that continues to this day, as well as a path of continuing to take all of my own work seriously.

I don't write for the purpose of being paid for my work (although that's certainly very nice when that happens!) but rather because getting my thoughts down on paper has for a long time been an important way for me to express myself. I do proofreading and editing for our family business and write book reviews for small journals. These jobs don't pay, but they are also a part of what I consider to be my work.

My paying job is another part of my real work which coincides with my area of interest. I work part time at a library. Though my job title is page—a position which traditionally involves the shelving of books—I actually process books, train new employees, answer reference questions, deal on a regular basis with our multi-cultural and

always unique patrons, and continue to use Inlex (our computer system) to search, catalog, and maintain records.

Many of my peers also are working for pay. More than a few of them work solely for the money and not necessarily because they enjoy the job or because it is representative of who they are. I am lucky in that I do enjoy my job, but it's not all luck that makes this possible, I've worked hard to find and pursue work that reflects how I see myself. My job is special to me because it's a part of who I am: a person who loves the literary world and sharing this love with other people.

When I help someone to find out about Molly Pitcher, I learn more about Molly Pitcher.

Every time I help a person who's uncomfortable with technology begin to understand the computerized card catalog, I invent and discover new ways to unlock the mystery. I deal with a wide variety of people in an ever-evolving range of ways. It's a challenge—and I love it.

I anticipate holding a lot of jobs (paid and unpaid) and doing a lot of work (formal and informal) during my life. I believe strongly that most or all will be as gratifying and as stimulating as what I'm doing now.

Karen McCabe, 35, teaches 3- to 6-year-old children at a private school. McCabe was a homemaker for eight years before returning to work to finance her children's education.

AFTER TWO YEARS of marriage and work, my husband and I decided to start a family. We had two children and I left the work force and became a full-time mom. Looking back now, it is rewarding to see the benefits of doing that and seeing how much stronger my son and daughter are because of it. I stayed home for eight years. When my kids were in school full time, I started thinking about going back to work. I tried two different kinds of jobs and could not stomach the corporate frenzy that everyone was busy with, so I followed my desire to work with children and applied for an opening at my children's private school. I was just what they were looking for and I felt so good to be needed. It was a perfect fit.

I love my job, 3- to 6-year olds are so honest and fresh. But I find that working with children requires a lot of patience. They work at a much different pace than adults. Children work at a task so they can learn something from it, while adults do a task just to get it done. Children have taught me many lessons in patience.

Children's sense of time is quite charming and I've had many conversations with them trying to sort out facts so I can understand what they mean. I smile a lot at work. Children are learning about life; they see or do something new almost every day. Everything is interesting—how fish eat, how a magnet works, using a broom or a sponge for the first time. If they make a mistake, they don't miss a beat. They just keep trying until they get it right. I draw much of my strength, humor, and confidence from the children in my class.

Since going back to work, I have learned creative cooking at home. There isn't a lot of time to prepare meals, so I have to be creative. I freeze a casserole and then put it in the oven in the morning on time-bake to cook so it is ready when we get home at night. I have also learned to clean my house in stages instead of the all-in-one-day method I used to have. I miss the freedom to go and do things as I want. I miss the free time I used to have for reading, crafts and sewing, but that's what retirement is for, isn't it?

I know that most parents are trying their best to be good parents and do the right thing, but it still breaks my heart to see children arrive at 7 a.m. barely awake with breakfast just wiped off their faces, and still see them there at 6 p.m. It is one of the downsides of working with children. I feel that children and their special needs are a forgotten part of our society and it makes me feel needed when I think of those 36 children at school. It is a privilege to work with them. I feel great about my job because I am doing my part to help the next generation. But my first job is to be a parent and I feel I am doing the best thing for my children now by being a "working mom" because I can provide them a quality education.

73

LaDoris Hazzard Cordell, 44, was the first African-American woman to become a state court judge in northern California in 1982. When she was admitted to Stanford University Law School in 1971, she was one of only two African-American women in the school.

DOLLY BELLAMY was 12 years of age when Abraham Lincoln signed the Emancipation Proclamation. Dolly, my great-great-grandmother, was a slave on a plantation in North Carolina. I have been told that during her 12 years of slavery, Dolly made several attempts to escape, seeking to find freedom in the North. My great-great grandmother's spirit could not be broken; she refused to succumb to the oppressive system of that era. My work on the bench is, in large measure, a tribute to the spirit and determination of this remarkable woman. As a consequence, I am dedicated to a judicial system that tolerates nothing less than fairness and justice.

When I was working in Mississippi in 1967, I met my first African-American lawyer who was a woman. To this day, I do not know her name, but she impressed me tremendously with her courage and commitment. Being inspired by her, and by my parents who have been my perpetual source of inspiration, I decided to embark on a legal career. When I was admitted to Stanford Law School in 1971, I was one of two African-American women in the school. There I was at one of the most prestigious universities in the country with my huge Afro, wondering if this

was where I should be. I found my professors to be supportive and understanding. Indeed, some remain my mentors and good friends to this day.

My decision to enter the judiciary was the result of my search for new challenges. I had practiced law for six years, establishing myself as the first and only lawyer in my community. During that six-year period, I returned to my alma mater, Stanford, to work as the assistant dean. In 1982 I became a judge. I wish that my grandparents could see me now. They were incredibly proud people, filled with dignity and high aspirations. But I do not think in their wildest dreams they imagined that their granddaughter would one day be a judge. When I get discouraged about the magnitude of social injustice or mourn the petty pace of societal change, I think about them.

When I first donned my judicial robe in 1982 at the age of 32, I knew that I wanted to devote the remainder of my career to being a judge. I feel comfortable in the robe—making a difficult custody decision or imposing a tough sentence in a controversial case. These are tasks I readily embrace. I continue to view my work on the bench as the greatest challenge of my professional life.

As the first African-American woman judge in northern California, and one of just a handful of women judges, the pressures upon me have been great. Not surprisingly, I have encountered the prejudices of those whose notions of how a judge ought to look, and what a judge ought to be,

clash with the image that I project.

Frequently, defendants appear before me, presenting themselves as victims of society. Sometimes, indeed, they are. Often, they are not. What they have in common is the expectation that they will be met by an older white male on the bench. When they see me sitting there, it is as if the entire system has opened up before them. The fact that I am African American and female lends enormous impact to my judicial persona. If someone like me can be a judge, then maybe the obstacles confronting them seem more manageable. I become the incarnation of their hope.

Judging is a complicated and complex task. So many skills and qualities are required to do this job well: analytic ability, reasonableness, integrity, punctuality. But these are only the fundamentals. Obviously, judges must do more. We must, when faced with laws and rules, and after considering the conflicting values and probabilities, make the most reasoned decision. We must do what we think is right.

The problems facing our judicial system are legion—the inadequate enforcement of child-support orders, plea bargaining in criminal cases gone awry, the lack of sentencing alternatives for drug offenders, our inability to deal effectively with drunk drivers, to name a few. I believe that it is as much the responsibility of judges to improve upon our system of laws, as it is to uphold the laws themselves.

I want to make a difference. At the same time, I desire to discharge myself of the debts I have accumulated to a system and a nation by which I have had the good fortune to be unusually favored.

Debby Gallie-Miller, 50, has been working as an outdoor guide and outfitter for 13 years. She is the only woman in the state of Washington who owns a horse-packing and outfitting business.

WORKING in a business that comes from a deep love within is both rewarding and fulfilling. I feel very fortunate to have been able to pursue my love of the outdoors and horses while fulfilling my natural tendencies to create and become a leader in my field. It is not always easy to follow your heart, work in a male-dominated field, and withstand criticism while breaking away from the traditional mold that has been set for women in our society. I have found that the most important quality to possess when following your heart is that of tenacity. Tenacity kept me going during sleepless nights whenever I doubted the dream that I was pursuing and when all the odds seemed stacked against my success.

My business is somewhat unique. The outfitting and guide business is operated under permit from the US Forest Service within our national forests. I hire, train, and manage a staff that takes the public into the backcountry on horseback to relax and enjoy the mountains. People come from big cities all over the world to share this outdoor camping experience and enjoy the wildlife, wildflowers, spectacular scenery, and untouched beauty of the Cascade Mountains in Washington. The experience allows them to discover more about themselves and build their self-confidence.

I have also developed a children's summer horse camp within the outfitting business called Camp Wahoo. This camp touches the lives of hundreds of children every summer, and teaches them to appreciate and respect the great outdoors and our public lands. The camp also helps kids build their self-confidence, share experiences with their peers, and develop trust, respect, and a sense of responsibility for their loyal companion, the horse.

The horses play a very important role in making the outdoor experience safe and memorable for our guests and campers. They are considered an important part of the staff and their attitude and behavior reflect the way in which they are handled and managed. The horse management part of the business is the most personally satisfying part of my job. The joy of watching the horses run free during their off-season helps me maintain a balance in life that sometimes gets lost among the everyday details of running a business.

When I first entered this male-dominated line of work, I was an employee of the business I now own. I found that my identity among my cowboy friends was not that of a peer. I was considered "the cook." This was an image that I planned to change. I was raised in a generation taught to believe that a woman's place is basically in the home, but to have training and be able to supplement your partner's income is "OK." Though I have always loved being at home, I seemed to gravitate toward people who had careers and like

Photo: Gary Kissel

interests. My experience running my own horse boarding and used tack and feed store, and managing a 70-stall boarding business, naturally lead me into the outfitting business. That first summer in the business, my children and I lead trail rides, saddled horses, learned to pack mules, mastered dutch-oven cooking over a campfire for groups of up to 25, set up camps, developed back-country skills, and performed first aid on people as well as horses. That summer was our most memorable time together as a family.

I have the only woman-owned, horse-packing and outfitting business in the state of Washington. I provide fully outfitted overnights in the high country, complete with dutch-oven meals, wranglers, and campfires. On our three- to-five-day pack trips, we move camp each night and travel through high mountain lakes and meadows. On our 90-mile horse drives, our guests assist in cattle round-ups. Now that I am married, my retired cattleman and auctioneer husband plays an active role in the business and shares my love for horses and the mountains.

Before I was married, I spent 17 years as a single parent of three active children. Although raising a family as a single parent is extremely challenging, it also was the driving force challenging me to pursue my love of animals and the outdoors. My business has brought me a sense of fulfillment, accomplishment, independence, and financial success, which in turn, has built my self-esteem and sense of self-worth.

Diane Bowman-Friend, 29, and her sister, Barbara Bowman, 27, work together running the family farm.

I HAVE ALWAYS loved working on the ranch, even though at times it drained me mentally and physically. My first years farming were interesting from the standpoint of "local community acceptance." Ironically, the worst opposition I had came from the local women (farmers' wives) rather than from the local men (neighboring farmers). I found myself really going out to these women, trying not to alienate them from me. Their acceptance was important in order to break down the barriers between the sexes. I feel that their daughters would not have an opportunity to do what I'm doing if their mothers portrayed me negatively.

I remember looking and searching for role models when I was young. At that time, there weren't many who chose careers in untraditional fields. My sister and I are fortunate that we were encouraged by our parents to get involved with the farm. There are six girls in our family, no boys, and I suspect that had something to do with Dad's encouragement. Quite possibly, a son would have gotten all my Dad's attention. Nevertheless, support and encouragement motivate people into areas they might not otherwise pursue.

Barbara and I have worked together all of our lives, but most seriously for the past two years. It's funny being adults now, working as colleagues, yet still enjoying the sibling friendship. We're very different from one another in some ways, such as personality, disposition, and opinions; but we have one common bond and that's this ranch. We feel an attachment to the land our Dad spent years building up and we feel a certain amount of responsibility to continue the operation successfully. The economics of farming have been lagging these past few years, but we're motivated by the future and what it holds.

Diane

THE MOST DIFFICULT part of working on the farm is when I can't do something …usually it's something that's either physically demanding or technical. I force myself to try, try harder to find a solution without running for my sister or one of the men to help me. It's not a matter of pride that stops me, it's a matter of accomplishing something on my own. I think women have a tendency to "give up" instead of pushing themselves to stretch the limits of their minds and bodies. I know I do, but if I'm going to be a successful farmer, I must compete with myself to attain greater self-confidence.

We are all conditioned through our adolescence to be "careful" or "don't worry, daddy will take care of you" or to "marry a nice man to

support you." But as an adult woman now, I want to face the world and its problems on my own, using whatever technique it takes to find solutions. I've found various solutions to the same problem, just by thinking creatively. The men I work with didn't understand my motives at first. They perceived my attempts as trying to impress them. After lots of dialogue of honest, heart-to-heart talks, we did come to a better understanding of me, them, and the issues that face women/men working relationships.

Barbara

Maria, 35, is a refugee who came to the United States to flee the war in her homeland, El Salvador. Thousands of civilians died in the civil war in this small Central American country. Maria is one of an estimated 300,000 Salvadoran refugees living in Los Angeles, and some 500,000 nationwide who fled their country in the 1980s seeking sanctuary and political refuge. She told her story in Spanish to the photographer.

EVERYDAY, seven days a week, Maria sells her wares on the downtown streets of Los Angeles, "*Un dolar!* One dollar!" Oftentimes for 11 hours a day she stands behind a box of socks, women's underwear, and cosmetics, each of which sells for about a dollar, hawking her wares and earning 25¢ to the dollar. During rainy weather she sells umbrellas. "I make about $100 a week as a street vendor when sales are good, and from this I must pay for food, rent, and transportation to work." She doesn't complain. She just tells her story. It is clear she is willing to work hard.

Maria left El Salvador after her nephew and brother-in-law had been killed by the government's National Guard. Her brother-in-law had been a union representative in the factory where he worked, and was killed for his organizing activities. "He was the strongest one in the family. His death hit us hard." She had to leave behind her 13-year-old son to be cared for by her widowed sister who also has children. One day she hopes to bring her son to the United States. But

so far, she has only been able to send $200 for her son, and she still owes money to the people in El Salvador who lent her money to leave the country. She misses her family, but does not plan to go back: "Life is hard and it is dangerous."

Maria has always been a vendor. While living in El Salvador, she sold chickens in the marketplace along with eggs laid by hens raised in the country. During the time she has been in the United States, Maria has had other jobs, among them cleaning offices 12 hours a day. But that job ended when the owner of the company never paid her $279 for her work—"He declared bankruptcy," Maria explains, although it is clear she knows this was not the truth. Next, she found a job selling newspapers and magazines, and then Spanish publications to passersby. But the city government soon made a sweep of the street vendors. Along with many other women, she was left without even the small wooden box she had used as her chair.

Since she is often sick, Maria would like to get a medical exam. She thinks she may have diabetes. She can barely see with her right eye and knows it is getting worse. Never having gone to school, she can read very little Spanish, but the letter she was given by the medical clinic is only in English. She hopes she may be able to get care in a few months. At times, she is depressed: "Life is very hard here, but I know I must keep on." She is sad to be so far away from her family, but along with the other women vendors, she laughs and banters as if they had no cares in the world.

Sons come to sit with some of them; friends or family often bring water or advance warning of an approaching police car. One would never know the sadness and tragedy behind the faces of this downtown street community.

Photo: Alberto Oropeza

Mary Byers Engle, 66, works at the Bailey-Boushay House in Seattle, helping people who have AIDS. Engle says that when she began this work, the very molecules of her being rearranged.

ABOUT THE TIME I retired in July 1992 I felt as if a magnet was pulling me toward volunteer work for people with AIDS. It almost seemed as if I had no say in the matter. I volunteered at Bailey-Boushay House, which is the first residential and adult day health facility in this country planned and built specifically for people living with AIDS. My job is to visit residents, parents, partners, and friends, and lend a hand wherever it is requested. I listen to life stories, hug, hold hands, and sometimes joke.

I had spent 14 years working at a mental health facility. I thought I had become accustomed to dealing with people who are hurting. But that experience had not prepared me for the spiritual impact of working at Bailey-Boushay House. I feel I've been getting ready to do this work all my life. Family, career, and volunteer work all helped. At first, I was unsure that I could handle the pain, sadness, and especially the ugliness of AIDS. I only knew that I had to try. Something inside of me insisted that I try to put my beliefs into action. Somehow I needed to create some sort of spiritual integrity for myself. It all came together.

Like so many others, my life has been darkened by AIDS—this disease that strips our culture of so much creativity and energy. A dear young friend of mine died of AIDS two years ago. At first, I felt like shaking my fist at the gods. I could not, and still cannot, imagine these human lives being wasted. After 18 months at Bailey-Boushay it dawned on me how blessed I am to be in such a sacred place.

All I can offer is an open and resilient heart. What I experience is one miracle after another. Each week I see the magnificence of the human soul: courage, hope, humor, and tranquility, when none of these should be expected. I look beyond the physical ravages of the disease and see God in these people. So many of these men, and increasing numbers of women, are giants of the human spirit. I find myself learning about real living from the dying.

I had no idea when I began this work that the very molecules of my being would be rearranged. I walk out of Bailey-Boushay feeling that I've been in a cathedral. I knew that in retirement I wanted to upholster my spiritual self. I had planned to study and take classes. How startling to realize my teachers are holy men and holy women, the residents who love me as they die.

There is no time for meaninglessness.

Photo: Sandra Hoover & Saul Bromberger

83

FACTORY WORKER

Rose M. Coburn, 53, worked at a rubber company primarily as a balloon stripper for about 25 years. In 1990, Coburn had to go on disability because of problems with her arms and hands, a condition called "over-use syndrome." At present, she is living off her small savings, raising chickens, selling eggs, and in a legal battle for worker's compensation insurance.

BORN AND RAISED on a 200-acre farm in Atwater, Ohio, I always worked in the fields with my father and helped with the cows, chickens, and pigs. Even after graduation from high school I preferred this type of work to an inside job. My father needed help, anyway. However, I knew that I would have to get a job sometime. I was a very shy girl, but in 1959 I went to Chicago where a friend got me a job in an exclusive flower and gift shop making $1.50 an hour. I became their head packer and gift wrapper in both the flower shop and gift shop, which sold a lot of fine china, crystal, and silver.

It was a nice enough job, and I gained much experience and made many good friends. However, this farm girl was never really content in the big city. My parents were getting up in years and I felt my father could use the help back on the farm. So, after five years I came back to Ohio. On Saturday evening after work at the flower shop I took off without telling my fellow employees, but I found out later they knew I was leaving. I arrived back home early Sunday morning and started working at the rubber company on Monday morning. Little did I know what I was getting into!

Although I worked in several different departments, most of my time was spent stripping balloons on the automatic balloon machine. Although it may look easy to a bystander, it is really a very hard job. It wasn't so bad several years ago, but like everywhere else, I guess, production has sped up and quality has dropped. Materials cheapened and so has the finished product. And no one seemed to care. I used to be able to take pride in my work, but then I felt ashamed to admit I had any part in its production. There were times when the factory had some of the work done elsewhere because labor was cheaper— meaning we didn't have strong unions and were offered few benefits.

It wasn't really what I would call gratifying work. It was just a job. Many trainees never make it, and many others have trouble with their hands and arms working the balloons on and off the forms, which results in much sick leave. I worked seven-and-a-half hours a day and was on my feet practically the whole time. Sometimes my legs and feet hurt so bad I couldn't hardly stand up when I got home. The factory got very hot at times, maybe up to a 100 degrees and they didn't have an air conditioner. All they had was an air maker that drew the hot air inside, and fans that blew in my face all day. I started at the balloon factory 30 years ago at $1.31 an hour, and was not even making $8 an hour when I left in 1990. I worked about 25 years when my arms gave out.

The muscles in my arms and my hands just gave out. The doctor put me through physical therapy for about three months, but it didn't do any good. The doctor just called it "over-use syndrome."

I got worker's compensation insurance while I was going through therapy. But after that, they just quit giving it to me, and I couldn't figure out from anybody why. That's when I finally hired an attorney. I had to go see more doctors, go to hearings, and for the whole year of 1990 I got nothing. In 1991, I got worker's compensation for awhile and then it stopped again. Right now, I'm not working. I'm just selling eggs, living on my small savings. Now I raise my own chickens and eat them. I raise most of my own vegetables, and sometimes my sister and I pick berries together. I don't feel so good now, and there's just nothing to make any money at.

Photo: William D. Wade

Kay Francis Albury, 44, is pastor of Ames United Memorial Methodist Church in Baltimore, Maryland. Albury and her assistant pastor, also a woman, try to bring hope into the lives of the hopeless.

THE GREATEST CHALLENGE I have is finding ways to communicate the gospel so that the church can make a real difference in people's lives. My church is in a community in great distress—people are suffering from drugs, unemployment, substandard housing, and low self-esteem. There is a real hopelessness among the people. It seems as if everything we're doing is not enough—like putting a Band Aid on a cancer. We have a soup kitchen that's really significant, but I always wonder when the people leave the church, will it make a difference? Will I ever see them again? We offer a worship service along with the meal, so we're feeding both the body and the spirit.

I had no idea I was going to be a minister, but I've been curious about the God/human relationships for a long time—ever since I was a child. My grandmother was a fundamentalist in terms of her understanding of judgment and that really had an impression on me. But when I preach, I don't tell people they need to know the Lord because of judgment day; I come from the opposite way and say it is because of God's love for us. I first felt the need to preach at the age of 23. I was working with Washington DC Manpower in a good-paying job, when I asked myself the ulti-mate question if there was more to life than my job. At the same time, I was involved with the life of the Methodist Church and I saw a group of young women who were former drug addicts do a song and witness. That was almost the turning point for me. I figured I didn't have those prob-lems, and if God could do that for them, who knows what God could do for me? It's been a spiritual journey of searching and wanting to be active in a church. I wanted to understand a lot of what we say in ritual and personally live that out.

My denomination ordains and appoints women. But it's one thing to be appointed, and another to be accepted. I've learned not to focus on the point that I am a woman, but that I am their pastor. I don't bring that as an issue, and if it's an issue, it's theirs, not mine. I have an assistant pastor who is a woman and she has been with the parish for a long time. In the beginning, one of the difficulties among my colleagues was the ques-tion of whether I was "tough" enough for such a job, especially a church with about 600 members. One person had allegedly said that, "Ames was a man's church." Well, it's been nine years now and I haven't discovered anything yet that's too hard to pray over, love, nurture, and grow with. It's been a great experience, and I'm looking forward to greater heights.

As a pastor, I want to offer people alternatives. Today people choose drugs and violence to deal with life issues, especially in the black community. I feel we have to address the issues that hurt and we often don't address those hard issues. There's some movement in the black community to build a coalition, but I also feel overwhelmed by the crisis of the black family and the community. We need to get people in the church to realize how much we are a part of each other.

I'm busy and have long hours, and over the years that has been a problem with my family. I'm a single parent with three children ages 21, 13, and 11. Several years ago, I lost another son to cancer. I worked out my grief by long hours and over-scheduling myself, but I've come to grips with that now. A lot of what I do is really left up to me. There are some meetings I must attend, but I can have fewer working hours and be more flexible.

In the final analysis, I believe that women bring a special "touch" to ministry, and we definitely need more black women in ministry. As women, we're given permission to say, "I don't know," or "I hurt," or "I'm afraid," which often breaks the barriers between clergy and laity. This often allows and nurtures relationships of reconciliation and love, whereby all involved can identify with their human, common struggle with brokenness and the need to be healed. The ministry is a very lonely profession unless we learn how to make friends and learn how to be nurtured and then to nurture others. As ministers, we often feel that we have so much to give to people, but people also have so much to give to us. All stand in need of being included, provided for, affirmed, forgiven and free to nurture their gifts all of the time. It's a continuous cycle of redemptive life.

Photo: George Holsey

Anthea Brown, 38, owns her own hat business, working out of a studio near her home. Brown often juggles her business with caring for her two young sons.

I LEFT my homeland, England, in 1974. We came to the United States, originally for a vacation, but decided to stay. In England I was an art teacher, but after a year I already felt institutionalized and depressed. Travel seemed the answer.

We found it difficult to get work in the USA without a green card. After my husband found a job in the antique business, and I had a few false starts, I decided to start my own business and go it alone. How I chanced upon the idea of designing and making hats, I don't really know. It came as a flash of inspiration after trying to think of something to do. Shortly afterwards, I opened my own hat shop in Venice, California. We were so poor that we lived in the back of the shop. We didn't have any babies right then, so it was all right. In fact, it was quite fun. Selling terrified me though.

A few months after I opened the shop, I took on a partner who was also a friend. She made clothes, so we decided to combine our efforts. I had never made hats before, although I'd been trained in art and design, which was a good basis. I found time spent in the sculpture studio very useful. The American public was most tolerant of my efforts and I learned my craft on them. Americans seem to applaud a tryer. In England,

we had this pinnacle of excellence constantly before us. It is both inspirational and oppressive. California is creatively very liberating.

Now, I have a studio in the building we call home. It's a much better life because I feel more in control. Our two sons aren't so small now and can tolerate being ignored for an hour or so. But the part of me that is a designer lives in the same body as the mother, and they are not good friends. All too often, when it gets down to the crunch, the mother wins and the designer feels cheated. Simon, who is 8, and Oliver, who is 6, will come into the workshop and sit down with me and draw. Then all the elements seem reconciled for a brief time. That is what I'm striving for, to tie all those parts of me together...to achieve autonomy.

You can maintain easily enough with children, but when you want to move ahead to accomplish something, problems arise. Right now, I am working on a fashion show. Sometimes, I feel like I am the teenager who has to be in by 10 p.m. when all her friends get to stay out until midnight. I was doing some work with a photographer who gets up at 11 a.m. and starts about 2 in the afternoon. His creative day begins about the same time mine ends.

My life constantly feels like coitus interruptus. There is little sense of completion. I am always having to scurry off, to walk out in the middle of things. We were doing some photographs in a lovely garden for the fashion show. There was great creative energy among us. We took a break

Photo: Margaret Grundstien

and had a picnic with champagne and strawberries. It was lovely. Then I realized, "My God, it's two! I have carpool." I had to leave right in the middle of everything.

I keep thinking that next week I will have more time, but next week comes and there is an endless new list of tasks to be juggled. I keep chasing my own tail. I have many more examples, but I have to go right now. I haven't got time to tell them all.

*Patricia Lawhon, 62, photographed with seven of
her ten daughters and one of her six granddaughters.
Lawhon is the mother of 13 children. She also teaches
at a local university.*

I AM THE HARDEST-WORKING woman
I know, always have been. A fact unglamorous
and immutable. As my 22-year-old daughter put
it, "You're so chore oriented." I like to think I
haven't time enough to finish all the projects I've
planned for this life. I can't be goofing off. The
truth, of course, must lie between these views.

Over 40 years ago, when I graduated from
college, I had vague career goals. It was war time,
and within a year I was married, had a husband
overseas, and was pregnant with the first of 13
children. I wallowed in the baby boom. (But not
in that throw-uppy "meet your husband at the
door in just a see-through cocktail apron" fool-
ishness.) What fed the fervor of domesticity?
Being Catholic and being an army wife. And I
never questioned the admirableness of either state.

Good friends shared my views. We wanted the
most attractive homes, the most achieving children, the most contented husbands, delicious
meals, delightful parties. We were neighbors on
army posts and we must have seen ourselves as
pioneer women crossing the plains together. We
worked our tails off, but never for money; that
would have been unthinkable. Our husbands
were officers, our children were young, we pulled
up stakes on very short notice. Our careers were

as army wives. I worked harder than most
because I had more to do—bigger quarters and
more children. Bridge parties, cocktail parties,
dinners—I didn't want to miss any. Of course,
they demanded that I return the invitations. I've
often thought I'm lucky that the things I most
like to do involve staying home.

What didn't we do! I turned out beautiful
clothes; learned to cover shoes with fabric at
Norfolk; refinished antiques; made fruit cakes by
the washtubful, planted flowers, made root beer,
ran PTA meetings and scout troops. We weren't
Pollyannas, but we thought what we did was
important and we did it well.

I work for money now. I teach at a Jesuit university, and I love it. I went back for a master's in
English (to counter the disorientation of quitting
cigarettes) and, by sheer chance, ended up teaching at a local junior college. Don't think this is
any big success story, though. At the university I
work full time, but no ability, enthusiasm, or popularity with students can change the status of a
non-PhD "lecturer." At my age, who would
bother with a PhD? I'd rather devote the time to
writing. I don't wish to cavil; I want women to
know you never get it all. If you put off a career
until you raise a family, accept the fact that you
are unlikely to catch up.

Almost all my children have graduated from
college. One daughter is a lawyer, another a
national park ranger. What I find surprising is
that six are nurses, especially since I want to bolt
when I see blood. My daughters claim I expected

Photo: Raisa Fastman

them to marry brain surgeons. I'm dead positive I never encouraged marriage at all. I do want them to have work they love. Women who spend their lives at work they hate are slaves. I tried to make housework creative—sheer numbers made a challenge out of motherhood. I love work, and I have a lot still to do. I'm writing a book and I have several new courses slated for next year. I just pray I have enough years to finish some of the projects I have in mind.

HAVING IT ALL: *Managing Jobs & Children*

NANCY L. MARSHALL, EdD

CAN YOU "HAVE IT ALL"? Can you have a job and a family and be relatively happy in your life? Often, television, movies, magazines, and newspapers suggest that women *cannot* be workers, wives, and mothers, or, if they try, they pay a price. Not surprisingly, the reality for working mothers does not look much like a TV show.

Women have been combining jobs and families for decades. The second half of the 20th century has seen dramatic social changes in the United States, especially for women in the work force. Spurred by the shift from a manufacturing economy toward a service economy, as well as by other demographic and economic changes, more and more women are holding paying jobs. While significant proportions of single mothers have held jobs throughout this century, with more than two-thirds of all single mothers employed in 1990, the rise in women's employment rates has also spread to married women with young children. While in 1960 less than 20 percent of married-couple families with children under six were two-earner families, by 1990 more than half of such families were two-earner families. Now, most working parents are faced with the complex challenge of managing children and jobs.

COMBINING WORK & PARENTING

Families face many challenges as they combine employment and caring for their children. Some have argued that individuals have limited time and energy, and adding extra roles and responsibilities creates tensions between competing demands, as well as a sense of overload and inter-role conflict. There is some evidence to support this; women and men who combine work and parenting sometimes do experience role overload and role conflict. However, not all individuals experience role conflict or strain.

The Center for Research on Women recently conducted a study of 300 two-earner couples, where both the man and the woman were working full time. About one in five parents reported that combining work and parenting did not create strains for them. When we compared parents and non-parents, we found that mothers' work-family strains are greater than fathers' work-family strains and greater than non-parents' work-family strains. However, we also found that both mothers, and women without children, reported greater benefits or gains from combining work and family than did fathers or men without children.

The level of strains or gains that parents reported depended on several things. Parents felt combining work and family was a positive experience when they had good jobs, when things were going well with their children, and when they had high levels of social support. In addition, mothers with less-traditional sex-role attitudes reported higher work-family gains. Parents reported greater work-family strains when they worked more than 35 or 40 hours a week, when they spent too much time on housework, or when they felt that parenting was too demanding or stressful. The study also showed that parents with high-prestige jobs were more likely to feel that work interfered with their family time. In addition, women with a child under the age of 12 were more likely to feel work-family strains.

While some parents do not report strains from combining work and family, and others find that the benefits balance the costs, those parents who feel strained by combining work and family are a reflection of the fact that our society has not kept pace with the changes in women's employment. There are several important supports from which all parents would benefit: changes in the division of labor in the family; societal support for quality, stable child care; and changes in the workplace, particularly increased flexibility and employer-provided child care benefits.

In the 1950s, when most mothers in two-parent families were home full time, they had primary responsibility for day-to-day care of the children and the home. However, when women began working outside the home, it was reasonable to expect that there would be some change in who does what around the house. In fact, men are doing more than they used to, although women still do most of the work around the house. National time-use studies found that, in 1960, married men's share of caring for children and doing housework was about one-fifth of the total time spent with the wife carrying the remainder of the housework load. More recent studies indicate that men are now contributing about one-third of the total time required for housework and caring for the children.

In the study of two-earner couples mentioned above, in at least two-thirds of the families with a child under 13, the mother has primary or total responsibility for planning, remembering, and scheduling day-to-day care of their children. While the mothers are the "planners," the fathers share supervising the children's activities in more than half of the families. Men share taking time off from work to stay home with a sick child in almost half of the families. However, making child-care arrangements for when the parents are at work is *still* the woman's task in three-quarters of the families.

Several studies have found that when husbands share in caring for their children, employed women are less likely to be depressed. In addition, one study found that when a father shares child-rearing responsibilities at home, the mother's employment is a more positive experience for the men. We found in the study of two-earner couples that both women and men report less emotional distress when the husband shares in supervising children's activities. The study confirms what working mothers in marriages already know—when men are involved in child rearing, their employed wives benefit. However, the research also tells us clearly that men benefit, too.

CHILD CARE & PARENTAL WELL BEING

Non-parental child care is crucial for two-earner couples. While some families can manage to combine child rearing and work through part-time employment or juggling parental work schedules, the majority of families use some form of non-parental child care. According to a study done by the US Bureau of the Census, three-quarters of children under the age of 5 whose mothers are employed, are in non-parental care. A little more than one-quarter of the children are cared for by relatives. A similar proportion are cared for by a family day care provider (a non-relative who watches children in her own home). Almost one in five are in nursery schools or child care centers, while only one in 20 are cared for by a babysitter or nanny in the child's home.

While non-parental child care is an important support for employed single mothers and two-earner families, some child-care arrangements are more supportive than others. As all parents know, child care can be a major source of stress. For many working parents, there are the everyday stresses associated with having a child in non-parental care: making lunches, getting children dressed and fed, and out the door.

There are also stresses that weigh more heavily when parents are concerned about the quality of care their child receives: is he or she getting enough stimulation, enough opportunities to play with other children, enough tender nurturing? Is their child physically safe, healthy, eating right, getting enough rest? All of these stresses and more can affect parents' well-being or feelings of emotional distress. In the two-earner couple study described above, we found that parents, men and women, who feel that their child-care arrangements do not meet their child's social development needs are more likely to be depressed or anxious. Conversely, parents whose children are in high-quality care that meets their child's social development needs are less likely to be distressed or anxious.

Child care can also be stressful when care arrangements break down, or when a provider is out sick or quits. Or those days when a child wakes up sick and there is no alternative child-care arrangement. Parents feel the tug between being the good parent and the good employee. In the study of two-earner couples, we found that men and women who feel that their child-care arrangements have been stressful recently are more likely to be depressed or anxious. However, men who do not share responsibility for making child-care arrangements report less stress about child care than do men who share the responsibility. For women, the majority of whom make the child care arrangements, sharing the task with their husbands doesn't reduce the stress. This suggests that exposure to the day-to-day vicissitudes of child-care arrangements (dropping off and picking up children, arrangements that break-down, providers and children who get sick, concerns about the quality of care, etc.) is the factor associated with child-care stress, rather than whether or not this task is shared.

WORK FLEXIBILITY & CHILD CARE

In addition to a more equitable division of labor, and quality, stable child care, parents' lives are also easier when they have flexible jobs. Researchers have examined the impact of flexible work schedules commonly known as flextime, and have generally found some positive effects. However, another study found that only 12 percent of workers in 1985 reported that they could vary the beginning and ending hours of their work. A

1990 study suggests that the level of flexibility is important. This study found that employed mothers of newborns who could change their starting and ending times on a daily basis reported lower work-family conflict, compared to those who could choose a work schedule but then had to keep that schedule for some minimum period of time.

In our study of two-earner couples, we found that workplaces varied in the degree to which they offered workers the flexibility to respond to nonwork situations. This variation is reflected in job satisfaction and work-family strains. Workers with more flexible jobs report greater job satisfaction, and reduced work interference in their home lives. Flexibility is associated with greater job satisfaction and reduced work-family strains for all workers—mothers, fathers, and women and men without children.

Employers can also provide important support to working parents through child-care benefits such as information about, and referrals to, available child care, help with paying for child care, and providing on-site child-care centers for the employees' children. Employer-provided child-care benefits may not only help employees and make it possible for women and men to manage work and family responsibilities, but they potentially benefit employers as well. In general, child-care benefits have been argued to affect the bottom line for employers through increased productivity and better worker morale, reduced turnover and absenteeism, improved recruitment, and an improved public image. The measurable benefits outweigh the costs, according to the cost-benefit analyses of 147 of the companies surveyed by the National Employer Supported Child Care Project in 1984.

To return to our original question, can you have it all? The answer is, yes, if you have a realistic picture of what it means to combine a job and a family. Will it be easy? That depends. First, we need the basics that everyone needs: a satisfying job, loving and communicative relationship with one's family, and strong social support from family, friends, and community. But families cannot do it alone. Families need high-quality child care, where children receive responsive, nurturing care, stimulation that is developmentally appropriate, and opportunities to learn about themselves and their world, and to develop relationships with other children and adults. Families also need stable child care, including backup plans for when child care is not available, or when a child is sick and can't go to the regular care arrangement. Finally, parents need support from their employers, including flexibility at work, and employer-provided child care benefits.

While this seems like a reasonable prescription, in fact, each of these supports is not yet available to many families. The lives of working parents will be improved to the extent that parents find such support from within their families, from their employers and from society at large.

Nancy L. Marshall is a senior research associate at the Center for Research on Women at Wellesley College. Marshall specializes in research on work and family issues, including studies of the impact of child care on children, working conditions for women, and the impact of work and family on women's health.

CHILD & FAMILY THERAPIST

Mary Demers, 38, works full time as a licensed therapist at a county children's shelter. She works on child-abuse cases, and reviews deaths of children under age 14 where there are strong indications of maltreatment. Demers has also survived the shock of making the transition from a homemaker to a full-time working mother. She wants to dispel the myth that working mothers are compromising themselves as caregivers to their families.

HAVING MARRIED at 19, I worked full time while my husband earned his degree and got a job with the fire department. Then I began my long journey through college and graduate school. During my eight years attending university classes, I had three children, now 10, 12, and 16. I considered myself a homemaker at the time because I was home all day with the kids, took care of the housework, groceries, and the daily grind of meeting the needs of my young children and our home. I attended classes three nights a week in the evenings. Dad stepped in to take over the baths and bedtime routine. The kids didn't seem to notice I was gone because "dad pretended he was a horse and we rode him around the house all night." Of course it was fun. All the work was done, the dinner was ready before I left so he could play with the kids, mess up the house, and knew I would be home to clean it up the following day. And that was OK, because I felt guilty leaving them at night and felt absolved the next day when I could clean up.

When I finished graduate school, I landed a full-time job a week before graduation that paid extremely well. I accepted the position and agreed to start a week after school ended. My excitement was short lived when the shock of this change became a reality for my family during my first week of working full time. If I realized then what I know now—which is that transition from a homemaker to a full-time working mom takes a well thought-out plan requiring everyone in the family to make adjustments—I would have started working a couple of days a week at first and slowly increased my time at work during the first month until our new routine settled in. There was no one to take over the daily needs of the family: chauffeuring, grocery shopping, house cleaning, and being there when one of the kids fell down and needed a hug.

At first I tried to do both jobs as a homemaker and working mother. I think the kids and my husband expected me to do both because I always had. When things got more and more behind, I finally called a family meeting to discuss and reorganize everyone's responsibilities and roles in an effort to bring back some order to the chaos and mess that seemed to take over our lives. It was during that family meeting that I realized how much change this meant for everyone in the family when I started working. The kids had some strong feelings and resentment about my not being home. For instance, my son Philip, then 7, said he didn't like having to go to day care because he couldn't watch his favorite TV shows

Photo: Steve Castillo

after school, and "the snacks at day care were crummy." We couldn't change the TV problem, but we had Philip list the snacks he'd like to have after school and we did our best to follow that list so he could bring his own snack. Jenny, then 10, said she hated having to go with other moms to her after-school sports games and missed having me drive to her class events. Dad and I agreed to drive her to at least half of the school events by scheduling the days ahead of time. After much venting and complaints, we put together a schedule that included everyone in the daily grind of keeping things going smoothly…so far, so good.

With my choice to work full time came the unplanned choice to give up certain things about being a homemaker I really enjoyed. As a homemaker, I had the luxury of being with my kids everyday and with that came a sense of competency and control. I felt adequate as a mom, and being available to my kids whenever they needed me reinforced my belief that a great mom is a mom who stays home with her kids. And I think this belief developed from my own childhood by having a mom who was a homemaker.

When I started working full time, I felt a tremendous loss over the relaxed pace I spent with my kids. Having the openness to do things as they came up, such as drive to school functions at the last minute, letting them have their friends over on any given day, or going to the library to check out any of the new children's books. These things now need to be scheduled far in advance. I seem to feel a time urgency once I'm off work to get the daily necessities done like housework, helping with homework, signing field trip slips, and keeping an adequate food supply in the house.

Out of this mini-crisis our family experienced during this time of transition, I learned two valuable things. One, I don't feel responsible to be a super mom to my family because it only creates a super monster. Breaking away from my image that "a good mom is a mom who stays home and takes care of her kids" was the most difficult struggle in my transition to be a working mom. At first I felt guilty and inadequate about not being there when certain milestones happened, such as school picnics or a basketball game where they made their first three-point shot. I usually tried to overcompensate for not being there by planning extravagant weekend outings or buying them something they wanted that I normally wouldn't do unless it was a birthday or Christmas. It wasn't until I realized that part of being a good mom is giving my kids the message that if I had a choice, I truly would be with them, but when it's not possible, I'm just as proud and love them just as much. I also don't need to make up for that time in any other way than to relive it over and over again when they tell it to me during dinner that night.

So my old belief has been replaced by a new belief that "being a great mom is a mom who works and loves her kids as much as any mom can." Also, every woman who makes the transition from homemaker to working mom goes through a crisis involving change for the entire family. I realized too that what I was going through was normal and, with a lot of structure, consistency, and predictability built into the family daily routine, this change could work. And now that I've been using this approach for the past five years, I can say that it's a good guideline in succeeding as a working mom. The only thing I continue to have difficulty with is the constant developmental changes my kids go through. The minute I think I got them figured out and establish a communication style that works, they give me that blank look as if they can't relate to a thing I'm saying.

As for my work outside the home, I specialize in providing therapy for children who are placed in a shelter as a result of abuse, neglect, or abandonment. My clients' ages range from 2 to 18 years old. They are referred for therapy because they suffer serious emotional problems such as depression, attention-deficit disorder, conduct behavior problems, and other more extensive psychiatric problems. Working with child-abuse victims, my work can often be two sided. There is the unpleasant and often disheartening side of dealing with the reality that innocent children are vulnerable by their innate trust of others. Children who have been abused are robbed of their innate trust and it may take years to recover. Knowing that I am participating in the healing process is the gratifying side to my work. Childhood allows children to be resilient in the face of trauma, heals their wounds of pain, and develops a healthy sense of self. As a therapist, my goal is to provide the most effective treatment for carrying the children through the tunnel of trauma and open them to a new life of trusting others again.

As a working mother, I feel good about my role as a professional and as a mother because it models for my children both my role as a working woman and my commitment to family life. It has taught each family member a cooperative effort approach to daily life, resulting in appreciation and respect for one another as a family.

Ruby Ling Louie, 62, has been a librarian for nearly 40 years, having served in public school and university libraries as a trainee, librarian, administrator, community researcher, library educator, volunteer supporter, and political advocate. Louie has specialized as a librarian for young people.

BEING A LIBRARIAN for the young has been more than gratifying in its calling. It has filled my life with endless good people to serve, always new things to find out for someone as well as for myself, and ever greater challenges in searching for ways to do things better for more people. This work is a *public service* and demands stamina. The pay will never be sufficient, so the constant reward is in the heart and soul, knowing that you have personally helped a part of humankind.

However, being a librarian for the young may become an occupation of the past in these complex days of the information super highway, but someone will have to pick up this joyous cross if humanity is to flourish. Most likely the work will first fall upon caring, literate volunteers, and ultimately it must rest upon individual nurturing parents and enlightened teachers, particularly women.

From the beginning, I was destined to be among the best of children's librarians. Born during the Great Depression to a struggling Chinese merchant and his reluctant pioneer wife from central Chekiang province, I was the youngest of three daughters. Unschooled, our exemplary mother was not told by the Cantonese women in Chicago's Chinatown that there was free education in America until one day when we were picked up by a truant officer. From then on, her children went to school in snow or shine. Now all her daughters would be educated as well as her precious son. Valuing learning, hard work, and giving of oneself to others were to be our way of life in the host country.

In the late 1930s, my parents stopped traveling annually with the World Fairs and opened several curio shops in China City, Los Angeles, so their children could attend school regularly. We lived in the central part of the city along with Italian, Mexican, Russian, Chinese, and Japanese newcomer families. No one else spoke our dialect, so English became our communicating language. Everyone was learning to become Americans together.

My gifted siblings went on to UCLA, but being the youngest and "average," no one was sure I needed to go to college. Then a blessed high school counselor suggested I try Long Beach City College. That way, I could wait on tables at the Chinese restaurant my parents had opened. I went to school there for four years, taking twice the number of classes to graduate. I took every course I could stay awake for, not knowing that this broad education would better prepare me for my future occupation as a librarian. By that time I was determined to graduate from UCLA and for the next four years I attended part time while

working at Ling's Cafe.

I still had not determined my major, but soon followed my second sister who was a master supervisor of teacher training. In my junior year, I regularly observed my sister training teachers in the university's elementary school library. My first mentor was an amazing librarian named Winifred Walker. Luckily, the following year, I had the opportunity to take a course in children's literature from the pioneer children's librarian, Frances Clarke Sayers. One class from her and I was hooked—I would become *her* kind of librarian. When I wanted to pursue my master's degree in

library science, Mrs. Sayers said the best place in America was Carnegie Institute of Technology in Pittsburgh because of Assistant Dean Elizabeth Nesbitt. She became my greatest pioneer master in children's work. This was the *best* year of my life—no work, and only well-rounded studies in all areas of library service—my soon-to-be true vocation.

In those early years, I had the opportunity to work and learn at the great New York Public Library. Eventually I returned to California and married an extraordinary Cantonese-American schoolmate who humbly shared his wife with her demanding career. We chose to live near China-town in central Los Angeles and raise our two children within an emerging immigrant community where we were spiritually comfortable. My first job was in South Gate with the County Public Library, administering to eight middle-to-low income communities of white and black children, helping to build strong book collections, as well as training the eager but unlicensed staff.

Among my many jobs as a librarian was my involvement in creating the Chinatown Branch Library. In the 1970s our small Chinatown community was being overwhelmed with extended families from Hong Kong because of the equalization of immigration quotas for Asia. My children's elementary school never had library services except for an occasional bookmobile stop. Thus, began a seven-year community effort that finally produced the Chinatown Branch Library housed rent free on school grounds. It was established through an arduous joint venture between city and school bureaucracies. As the resident librarian, I was the founding president of a unique support group of extended community activists who worked to establish this library.

For the past five years I have been privileged to serve one of the finest library media centers, which is located at the nation's largest middle school located in South Gate, California (my old workplace). We serve 4,000 students on a year-round basis. In collaboration with our co-librarian, Dale Buboltz, we have developed the ultimate in library service for young people. There are two teaching librarians on call throughout each school day, and I, with a full book bag, regularly visit classrooms on our "Reading Road Show" program to promote reading aloud, language and communication techniques, great books, and above all, the many joys of becoming a lifelong, autonomous reader.

Kathy Williams, 36, has been working in shipyards since 1978, mainly building ships. One day she hopes to expand her welding talents for creating art sculptures.

IN GRADE SCHOOL I had the usual dreams of a young girl. I wanted to be a school teacher, veterinarian, live with my best friend in the woods, and work at the steel plant not far from my school.

At 13 I began to drink and take drugs; it hid the differences between me and the other girls. It wasn't until I was 17 that I realized why I felt apart from my girlfriends. I was what was called a dyke, butch, a lezz. My mother was the first person I told. She was very understanding for when she was younger she lived with several gay men. She learned that it was not a lifestyle they chose. But, of course, she hoped it was a phase I was going through.

At 18, my childhood dreams were forgotten. I could no longer hold down a job because of my alcohol abuse. I moved to the city where rent was cheaper and all the bars were within stumbling distance. I soon discovered that men were willing to pay for my services. I had convinced myself that because of my sexual orientation I would not feel used; that I would be in control. So began my life as a prostitute, with my goal to drink enough alcohol to pass out every night and begin again in the morning. A couple of years later I really hit bottom. A man refused my services, and all I was asking for was one drink.

I moved in with my mother and signed the waiting list for a school a friend had told me about. I was going to become a welder and get paid for learning. Even though I had no idea what welding was, I began school eight months later. I met my ex-partner of seven-and-a-half years in my class. We both finished school, took a welding test at a welding car manufacturing company and passed, starting there at over $8 an hour.

I drank all through school, before, during, and after. But once I got the job, I only drank after work, and, of course, on the weekends. After a year and a half with the company I went to a 21-day treatment center. I remained sober until the company closed about eight months later. My partner and I were always open about our relationship. Neither of us ever received any kind of harassment because of our sexual orientation or because of our sex. We were both good welders and most importantly, we had a great sense of humor.

I then took a test at a major shipyard, passed and was Navy certified. What a difference shipbuilding was! I had to carry heavy welding leads and portable welding wire machines up ladders to get to my job. I froze in the winter, got wet and shocked when it rained, and felt as if I was in a sauna during the summer. I loved it! Once again I quit drinking and I began working out with weights before work. Being a woman, I felt I always had to prove myself to my co-workers, even though I've heard more than one leadman state that the women usually are better welders—

Photo: Gary Kissel

they work harder, don't miss as much work, and learn quicker.

Once again I was open about my sexual orientation and had no conflicts with the men. But I have to admit that I stayed out of the women's locker room. I was not comfortable when the women changed in and out of their work clothes. I was fearful of a homophobic woman making charges against me. To be honest, sometimes I have a harder time with the women. At that time, most of the women were laborers. When they discovered that I was a welder, I immediately felt their resentment, as if I felt superior, which was

not the case. I have respect for everyone who works hard.

I was involved in a serious accident at work in 1985 and I almost lost my lower left leg. Due to my injuries, I could not return to welding. Since my accident, my life has changed. I tried every job that my ninth-grade education could get me. I tried being a nurse's aide, security guard, taxi driver, and hotel maid, just to name a few. I went from making $13.90 an hour to barely over $5 an hour.

Several years ago my sister left her husband of 15 years. My sister and her five children stayed with me for a few months until she got her own place. My oldest niece who was 13 at the time decided to stay with me. Later, my 11-year-old niece came to stay. I have been fortunate that my partner of four years has been understanding and patient with me. It has been a wonderful experience to be a part of the girls' growing up.

In the summer of 1993 I again enrolled in a tech college to re-learn welding. My welding skills quickly returned and I rejoined my union, the Boilermakers. I took a test and passed, and I began working the weekend shift at a shipyard. I continued to go to school to learn new welding processes for job security and to make $21 an hour or more. I have to admit that the work was harder than before, the leads seem heavier, as do the machines. But I can't imagine doing any other; to me welding is fun and it's an art.

SOCIAL ACTIVIST

Bette Shertzer, 49, has spent all of her adult life work-ing for social change and ways that people can live and work together harmoniously. Shertzer has been involved with organic-food co-ops, a collectively run bakery, and a cooperative association with farmers and consumers.

OVER THE YEARS my need to work for social change has taken me many places with many vocations, but always with the inten-tion to see how people can live together in freedom with dignity and respect for each other's differences.

I began as a '60s activist demanding justice—human and civil rights for all people. After those difficult years, I reflected on "what went wrong," and realized that the struggle had to go deeper. The struggle must be reflected in ourselves—in the way we live our lives, right down to the way we think about things. I began to see that we needed to do more than just talk and make demands. We needed to create alternatives that allow people to see that it is possible to live differ-ently and structure our lives on a different basis.

I became involved in organic-food co-ops. I also got involved in land and worker issues, such as who controls land, the loss of small farms, migrant and cannery worker situations, and more. This led me to On the Rise Bakery in Syracuse, New York, a collectively run, whole-grain organ-ic bakery where the workers shared all the work, except for the deliveries, which we slowly gave to a friend to handle. I came to see deeper connec-tions between my inner self and my work, and how one should reflect the other. I felt I needed to put my ideas into practice to see how they held up in reality and work at a physical job using my whole body, not just my mind. I wanted work that "centered" me, challenged me, and at the same time, showed people that alternatives do exist and can succeed if we are committed to work hard and creatively with one another through ups and downs.

The years at the bakery were invaluable for me. Not just in offering people good, healthy food but in how we worked together to do this. I worked with five to seven women, depending on the work load. We were very different people, but the one thing we had in common was our commitment to the bakery and its products. Our decision making was by consensus and although it was often a difficult and time-consuming process, it is one that I feel will be used much more in our society. Consensus allows for every opinion to be heard and considered. And yet, each person had to weigh how important her position was on an issue. Over the years each one of us did at times stop a decision because it was not something she could work with. This process demands that the individual be clear about her own position but also keeping in mind that we work respectfully with one another.

During my years at the bakery I read the work of a philosopher, Rudolf Steiner. Steiner lived at the turn of the century and spoke of the spiritual forces behind all physical existence. His writing

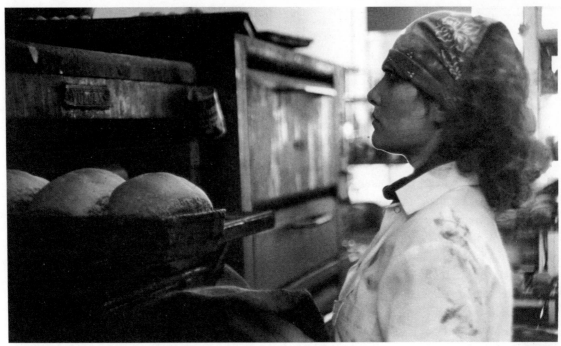

opened up greater horizons and challenges for me. After seven years at the bakery, I decided to leave and move on to a 400-acre dairy farm that was part of a community founded by people who, inspired by the ideas of Steiner, wanted agriculture, education, and the arts to interweave closely within their community life. But even in this community, founded with clear social ideas, there is still much work to be done on how people work together.

I am now involved with a small group of people who try to use Steiner's ideas to create work situations. Based on this philosophy, we recognize that as human beings we are all equal and share common laws to ensure equal treatment of one another. Also, through our individual strivings, there must be complete freedom to reach our potential. Lastly, in the economic realm, we all need to work for one another so that each of us can have what we need to survive. Out of these thoughts we have formed the Harlemville Community Economic Association, which started as an association where farmers join with consumers to reach agreement on what crops will be grown and what the price will be for a season. Farmers and consumers then enter into contracts before the season begins, thus ensuring a market for the farmers and food for the consumer at mutually agreed-upon prices. We see this as expanding into other areas of life as well, so that we can come together not as each person trying to make a living (at times at the expense of others) and learn how together we can each receive what we need in order to live.

CITRUS PACKER

Lupe V. Reyes, 54, began packing oranges when she was 16 years old.

TO WRITE about myself is hard for me to do. I don't have much education because I had to quit school when I was young.

I had lots of brothers and sisters to care for because my parents were not well. Being second to the oldest, I had to help out. At 16, I started working in a packing house packing oranges, and have worked in packing houses a long time. Oh, I have gotten other jobs, but it was not the same. So, I would quit and go back to the packing house. We work hard, but it is a good job.

When I first worked in oranges, it was for Blue Goose Packing House. I think we got 10¢ a box, but then the work was much harder. The way we packed the oranges was different and we used big wooden boxes that had a wooden divider in the middle. We didn't set these boxes on the line like we do today, but on small benches we had at our station. In the box we put 113 oranges on one side and 113 oranges on the other side. But the hard part was to wrap each orange in tissue paper and the little goose on the paper had to go right in the center so it looked good.

We could pack about 100 boxes a day, so maybe I would make $12 for the day. Now we use cardboard boxes and best of all, we don't wrap the oranges any more. The boxes are smaller so we can work much faster and make more money. We get about the same amount of money we did when I started in the packing houses, but now we can pack more. We get 12 ½¢ a box, and our minimum is 220 boxes a day. Lots of times, if you are strong, you can pack 220 boxes in the morning, and if you are still strong or young, you can do the same thing in the afternoon. If you don't make your minimum, the packing house pays minimum wage—they have to by law.

Oranges come in different sizes and we pack them that way, such as the small orange is a #210 because 210 oranges fit into the box. The largest orange is a #48 because 48 large oranges go into one box. In the packing house there are different lines with different size oranges on each line. We work each line 15 minutes, packing different sizes because we are paid by the box, and if we only pack small oranges, we would not make any money. So we change so that everyone gets a chance to pack the different sizes and make more money. The packed orange box weighs between 46 to 50 pounds each, and we each pack between 300 and 400 boxes a day. If we could pack 48s all day, I would be rich.

Now that I am older, I'm glad I don't have to lift the boxes very far. And I don't want to work 12 hours anymore. Being an orange packer is fun and it has its advantages because it is seasonal. I can be home with my kids in the summer. I am the mother of four and the grandmother of 14, so they don't have to stay with someone else. I really like my job and most of the other employees, and our boss is good to us.

Yoshie A. Cooper, 48, builds models of complex structures prior to their construction.

BORN AND RAISED in Japan, my technical career started in Tokyo as a tracer. Under the Japanese labor system, both male and female employees start at the bottom level and work their way to the top. One must go through all the aspects of training. No short cuts, regardless of superior abilities. Thoroughness and neatness are most important in Japanese business. This system doesn't permit fakers and freeloaders. I was somewhat of a maverick because I soon left the Japanese employer to work for an American architectural firm that was doing designs for the United States Defense Department. I did architectural drafting under American and Japanese supervisors.

There was no resentment against women in the US firms operating in Japan. Opportunities and rewards were there according to ability. In the spring of 1964, I married my American architectural supervisor, and in the fall of that year, migrated to the United States. I spent two years studying English at college, adjusting to the culture, keeping home, and raising flowers, and building structures for the garden. I loved the "do-it-yourself" lumberyard and the "do-it-yourself" tools, which gave me the courage to build two houses during the 1970s, from excavation to wallpapering.

After two years in the US, my former office asked me to work as an architectural draftsperson. This was my first encounter of freeloaders and fakers. There wasn't the old pride of workmanship that I had experienced in Japan. I soon discovered supervisors played favorite to some employees. They were usually the employees who had a "gift of gab." Being the boss's favorite in the US doesn't mean you're the best qualified. In Japan, if you are a favorite, the entire company supports you as an exceptional employee.

In 1974, after 15 years of architectural drafting, I saw a newspaper ad for a piping designer. I applied for the position to be trained and was accepted. The work in piping was more gratifying than architectural drafting. I received the same treatment as the men even though the ratio of female pipers is one to every 60 men. Projects are usually large and are needed posthaste. Consequently, there is a lot of rapid hiring and rapid layoff. This is not good for personnel morale. It would be much better if we could diversify our experience, then we could work more efficiently with less people and wouldn't have the big layoffs. A family attitude is better than the factory job attitude.

Piping design model making has proven to be very helpful for the industry. Many of the petrochemical, sulfur, and nuclear plants are so large and so complex, that the color-coded model designs are effective in eliminating interferences and are easy to visualize and understand. There are fewer design glitches when you build a scale model. I always enjoy working with my hands and I have the patience for tedious details. When people ask me what my occupation is, I say, piping designer. Ten out of ten people reply with the question "What?" Then I have to spell p-i-p-e, piping designer.

In 1993, after finishing a big model project, I received a layoff notice due to company downsizing and restructuring. For the past decade, client requests for 2-D and 3-D Computer Aided Design (CAD) has had a major affect on the architectural and engineering profession. The need for CAD operators is greater than that for model makers. Slowly but surely electronics and keyboard crunching will completely replace the hands-on techniques of plastic-model making, the flowing strokes of a drafting pencil, the character of line work and lettering, and the pride of product. The old techniques have such warmth and personal character that many works could be framed and hung on the wall.

While progress must go on, I am sorry to see the loss of the old arts. I truly believe that one day, all too soon, pencils, erasers, and triangle scales will be found only in antique shops.

Photo: Candace Allen

Linda Bonder, 30, works for a computer technology company in Portland, Oregon. She recently took a year-long hiatus from work for travel and reflection.

THE IMPORTANCE OF a successful, professional work life has always been deeply ingrained in me. When I was a kid, my parents had their own accounting business and an intense commitment to their work. I knew that we had nice things and opportunities because of my parents' hard work and long hours. I grew up understanding that everything I did required a sense of ownership, commitment, and pride.

I never questioned that hard-work ethic. High school was fairly easy for me, but I still studied hard to get top grades. I got accepted to Princeton University and earned my bachelor's degree there. Even then, the business mentality was so much a part of me that I majored in economics without seriously considering any other departments. After Princeton, I went directly to the Massachusetts Institute of Technology (MIT) to get my MBA. My class at MIT was 23 percent foreign students—but only 20 percent women. Being in the minority didn't phase me. If there was discrimination, it was subtle and I didn't notice it.

After business school I started working at Intel, a high-tech company in Portland, Oregon. My first job was doing technical customer support over the phone. There were several women in my group, but we were clearly a new breed for some customers. We all heard some men say, "Honey, I sure hope you can help me," or "Thank you, dear." One male caller insisted that I didn't know what I was talking about. I passed the phone to a male co-worker who solved the caller's problem by just repeating my advice.

Fortunately, being a woman did not pose any problem within Intel. Over time, I moved up and over into jobs that I enjoyed more and more. After three years, I became a product manager for a line of computer networking products. I was responsible for marketing, customer satisfaction, and other factors that drove profits and losses. My decisions affected customers, engineers, manufacturing people, and sales teams. I loved the responsibility and the stimulation of working with so many different groups. I took pride in doing a good job not just for my paying customers, but for my internal customers, the people within Intel who relied on me for input and information.

The flip side was that I became frustrated because so many people needed my time. Between answering telephone calls, responding to electronic mail, and attending meetings, it was often difficult to be productive during business hours. On some days, I turned off the ringer on my telephone just so I could concentrate on writing a proposal or presentation. I did my most intensive work after 5 o'clock. Staying until 6 or 6:30 didn't bother me, but I hated working more than 50 hours a week unless there was an exceptional reason.

A co-worker once gave me a quote which I always try to remember. I interpreted this quote as a message to balance my life between work and self.

Often people attempt to live their lives backwards: They try to HAVE more things, or more money, in order to DO more of what they want, so that they will BE happier. The way it actually works is the reverse. You must first BE who you are, then DO what you need to do, in order to HAVE what you want. —Shakti Gawain

Then an unexpected accomplishment started changing my perspective. While skiing in Utah in 1991, I accidentally found myself on a more difficult slope than any I had ever skied. When I got to the bottom in one piece and decided to do the run again, a light went on in my brain. If I could do that run and enjoy it, maybe I should rethink other experiences I had passed over. That spring, I successfully climbed Oregon's 11,200-foot Mount Hood. Three months later, I ran 17 miles in a team-relay race. Each experience was an eye-opener for me.

During that year, I saw new meaning in the quote. I felt that to *be* myself, I needed to do more things purely for myself. That realization led me to take a break from my career. My husband and I had often talked about taking a year off work, but I had never been able to picture doing it. By the end of 1992, I was ready.

The year off work was more rewarding than I had hoped. We spent most of it hiking and backpacking through the Canadian Rockies, Alaska, Nepal, and New Zealand. We also visited Israel, Thailand, and Malaysia. We spent a lot of time with our families. I learned a tremendous amount not only about the people and places we visited,

Photo: Angela Pancrazio

but also about my personal abilities, values, and goals. I learned through challenging myself physically—backpacking over steep mountain passes in Alaska, and hiking up to 18,000 feet in Nepal. I also learned just by spending time alone without the brain clutter of work.

I was rewarded by a strengthened understanding of who I was and what I could accomplish. I reaffirmed that a challenging career was important to me. I recognized that to enjoy my career over the long haul, I had to balance it with my personal life. And I finally understood that to achieve a true balance, I needed to set significant personal goals and stay committed to them.

Now I'm back at work and trying to keep my work week down to 50 hours. It's a challenge to be in my old environment while learning to integrate new discoveries into my life. But now I know how important they are, and I'm determined.

Mary Anderson, 64, lives in a first-aid station atop an 8,000-foot mountain. She has been caretaker of a mountain ski resort in the summer and on the ski patrol in the winter for the past 17 years.

I LOVE THE MOUNTAIN. Since I have been here, I can't think of a place I would rather be. I love to do things to keep it beautiful and a pleasant place to be. The mountain has been good for me. The things I do can be called a labor of love. The hikers and skiers, young and old, summer and winter, reflect the spirit of well-being and ecstasy. They tell me how they wish they could have a job like mine.

I feel comfortable with challenges, testing myself mentally and physically, finding new strengths, and being able to tackle the almost impossible tasks without the aid of man or machine. Feeling no fear in being alone while Mother Nature does her thing...blinding blizzards, wind, rain, lightning, bugs. I live with the bare necessities up here on the mountain with running spring water, a gas refrigerator, and a generator for electricity, although I prefer a kerosene lamp for light. I like the feeling of getting along without civilization's comforts and living a simple life. The more things you have, the more there is to do and worry about. I've lived out of a backpack long enough to know how completely free you can feel from mundane, boring, daily living. One of my favorite quotes is Ellen Burstyn's: "What a lovely surprise to discover how unlonely alone can be."

Before coming to the mountain 17 years ago, I was married and worked in the Los Angeles garment district as a seamstress and designer's assistant making expensive designer clothes. I skied every chance I could, and one night I said to my husband, "What I'd like to do is retire from my job and turn into a ski bum." I signed up for ski mountaineering training, became a professional ski patroller in 1973, and joined the staff at a nearby ski resort. I took a survival course after becoming a ski patroller and spent five weeks with the bare necessities in the wilderness, walking 350 miles. After that, I felt like I could lick my weight in wild cats, and that I was one leg into developing myself for the outdoor life.

My husband divorced me after 39 years of a good marriage and left me destitute. We lived an upper-middle class existence with the nice home, swimming pool, and all the things that everybody dreams of having. Since then, I have learned that I can accomplish things by myself and I have faith in myself. Now, I feel great being on the mountain. I have four grown children and 19 grandchildren, so I'm on the telephone a lot. The one difficulty of my mountain home is that when my family wants to visit, there's no place for them to stay; and I no longer have the swimming pool and the trampoline for the grandchildren that came with the nice big home.

In winter, I spend my days on the slopes keeping watch for injured skiers, and providing emergency medical care if necessary. Just before dark

Photo: Walt Mancini

each day, we do a sweep of the slopes to make sure all the skiers are accounted for and no one is lost. Sometimes I forget I'm an old lady because I don't have any aches and pains, not the way I used to before I got into skiing. I love the cold, the pure air, and the drinking water. I think that's what keeps me healthy. In my spare time I like to stay creative. I sew and put quilt tops together with a treadle sewing machine that works like a charm.

The owner of the ski lift has encouraged me and trusts me in my job. A man who can recognize a woman when she does something good and acknowledge it is a real man—and that sepa-rates the men from the boys. You never know what's going to happen from one day to the next up here, that's why I love my life. Sometimes, I think it's almost miraculous the way that I feel!

*Ana Torres Cross, 36, manages a 50-person depart-
ment of software engineers with a budget of more than
one million dollars a year at Hughes Information
Technology Corporation. Cross studied engineering in
college, and worked her way up the job ladder to her
present position.*

OUR CUSTOMER has one million dollars
he wants us to spend on software upgrades
next year in addition to our normal operations
and maintenance contract. Where do I find the
staff to spend it? And if I don't agree to spend it,
how will that affect our future business opportunities?

One of our system administrators (SA) is looking at other opportunities outside the company.
How big a raise can I afford to offer him to keep
him? How will his raise affect the morale of the
other SAs?

My 3-year-old son's behavior and lack of
respect for boundaries is jeopardizing his future in
day care…now what? Speech therapy; focused
behavior modification; more time (from where?)
with Mom and Dad.

Some mornings I wake up and wonder if this
is really my life. I am 36 years old and I manage a
50-person department of software engineers with
a budget over one million dollars a year. I have a
husband, two sons, ages 7 and 3, and a stepson
struggling through his first year in college.
Through the grace of God I make it through
every day, but without the support of my ever-

faithful husband, and a wonderful and understanding boss, I know I wouldn't be where I am
today.

I look back on a life that started in a row house
in New York, and where the growing years took
place near a barrio in southern California. My
mother had a very hard life and *always* told us that
getting an education was much more important
than having a family. School first, kids later.

Being the oldest of four girls in a Puerto
Rican family meant that I had the responsibility
for setting the example. My parents had high
expectations and I was determined to meet them.
I graduated eighth out of 600 students from high
school, and picked engineering as my major in
college. Only one other female in our large,
extended family had made it through college, but
I was too stubborn to quit without giving it a
shot. I was good in math and I'd heard that engineers were highly paid, so without any real vision
of what to expect, I went off to college.

Being female and Hispanic in a non-traditional
field (engineering) gave me more than just technical challenges. Being harassed and ostracized by
my male counterparts was a part of life in college
and even continued into the workplace. I was
hired by Hughes Aircraft as an engineering student after my first semester in college because of
my 3.6 GPA. As I continued to struggle with my
studies and my identity in a white-male world,
my GPA spiraled downward. I ended up married,
divorced, and finally switched from mechanical to
electrical engineering. The work was more

my identity comes from being His child. I'm where He wants me to be and if I follow His plan, it will work out better than I could imagine. With a huge sigh of relief, I started confronting the people who indulged in the harassment. I earned a reputation for being fair and not putting up with anything less than professional behavior from *anyone*. I've worked my way up the ladder to finally find myself leading this department.

Part of my daily challenge includes setting a standard where people are treated according to what they contribute in the workplace—not their color, size, gender, familial status, and so on. I am part of a company-wide diversity team and our focus is on helping people get beyond what they "see." I am often called to facilitate and mediate work-diversity issues, and will be personally involved with the company-wide diversity training as a trainer.

My main responsibility now is to get the "stuff" out of the way and procure the resources my people need to get their jobs done. Operating and maintaining one million plus lines of code while being on call to support our customers and users is no small task. I provide the leadership and vision necessary for my people at work and my family. I find peace in knowing that I'm right where God wants me to be—putting His agenda before mine and serving those around me.

appealing and I'd found a mentor to help me through the rough spots. Six years after I'd started college, I finally graduated.

My second husband dragged me to Colorado in 1982 where I was finally able to settle down and seriously focus on my career at Hughes Aircraft. Unfortunately, the treatment I received from my white, male co-workers was almost intolerable. The innuendoes, the constant, degrading comments and berating had me seriously doubting my future. The Lord played a big role in my life here because just when I decided I couldn't take it anymore, He reminded me that

IMAGE CONSULTANT

Darlene O'Farrell, 45, works with women interested in improving their physical appearance from head to toe.

I NEVER INTENDED on becoming an image consultant but have always been drawn toward working with women in the fashion industry. It started when I was a single parent and needed an education. I went back to school and took fashion merchandising. I loved the creative part and it seemed there were so many different aspects to fashion that I would never get bored.

As a child growing up, my parents never encouraged me to get an education let alone have a career. I know they did the best they could, but a college education was never talked about. My goal in life was to have children, be a housewife and live happily ever after. I loved being a mother and raising my children, but in the 1980s, women became career women. As a housewife, I felt inadequate. My children were growing up and I wanted to improve myself and be a productive person in the work force.

I've done many different odd jobs and most of them have been working with women and related to fashion. The one thing that stood out most was that the women who were happy and secure with themselves were the ones that were beautiful on the outside. I wanted to become one of those women but I wasn't sure how to do that. I've spent the last 15 years of my life working on bettering myself and I've been able to share that with other women, and that feels good.

I started working with the American Cancer Society's "Look Good, Feel Better" program about two years ago. My mother died of cancer when I was 19 and I always wanted to volunteer for the Cancer Society. It took me 24 years to do that and I had a lot of fear and little confidence. As an image consultant I learned to work with women on their image from head to toe. I always thought makeup seemed less important until I talked to cancer patients and they said that makeup was the one thing that made them seem normal when they were going through cancer treatment. I love working with women and being their friend. They have brought so much into my life and I know I've brought some self-confidence and beauty into theirs.

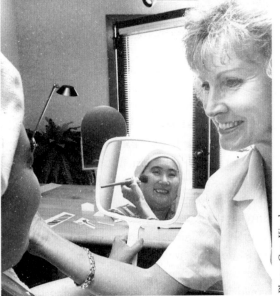

Photo: Gary Kissel

Christine Choy, 38, has made about 45 films, and her work has been recognized with an Academy Award nomination, Peabody, and Columbia du-Pont awards, among others. Choy also teaches at New York University's Tisch School of the Arts.

WHEN I WAS BORN, the world was changing dramatically. The Korean War was ending, the Cold War was beginning, and the People's Republic of China was under the full swing of Chairman Mao's leadership. Shang-hai, the city in which I arrived, didn't welcome me with open arms. I was not an ordinary Chinese child, with my mother's Mongolian blood and my father's Korean nationalism. In addition, I was not the first born, and more importantly, I was not a boy.

Soon after, my father left permanently for Korea and so I was entrusted to a family of all women: my mother, my maternal grandmother, my sister, Ah Ma (an old maid who took care of my mother), and Ah Mei (who took care of my sister and me). As far as I could tell, they all hated me simply because I was a girl. Out of revenge, I became a tomboy but excelled in my schoolwork. All the neighbors and school teachers liked me a great deal, telling my mother what a charming daughter she had. But at home, I invited endless spankings from my grandmother because I refused to be docile and obedient while she told me a million tales about what is good luck and what is bad luck. I called her names too. So under

these conditions, I grew up with a philosophy that I must become somebody so my family would eventually pay me some respect. Though, even to this day, my mother still doesn't understand what I do.

After nine years in China, my family moved to Seoul, South Korea, where my father was living. I immediately disliked the country. My mother could no longer work because it was considered shameful for a man to send his woman to work in public. So my mother became a neat freak, always cleaning and straightening the house. My grandmother stopped talking altogether, spending all day, everyday, cooking, and worrying about whether my father would like her multi-ethnic cuisine—a mixture of Mongolian, Chinese, and Korean delicacies. I just tuned out the family feuds and went to the movies every weekend, read a lot of books, and ate less and less until I ended up bedridden in the hospital.

In 1967, my mother saw a picture in the Asian edition of *Life* magazine. She excitedly told me that I ought to go to the United States and enroll myself into a Catholic women's college because that's what the future empress of Japan had done. I applied and got a scholarship and a one-way ticket to America. I arrived in New York with a letter of introduction and $60 in my pocket. The school was very wealthy and white, and few people paid much attention to me. But I did make a few friends. They were a few years older but I suppose they took pity on me. When they left school, I decided to leave as well.

With no money, no connections, no relatives and no friends, I worked and worked to make money for living expenses and to continue college. Over the next few years I studied architecture at Princeton and Columbia. Throughout that time I worked at Alexander's department store, modeled for a photographer until he tried to take advantage of me, babysat for many wealthy families, and finally landed a job at an architecture firm. The boss liked me so he asked me to move in with his family to be a companion to his not-so-pleasant son. One night, he sneaked into my room, I screamed. The next day I moved in with another family to take care of their two spoiled kids. I decided to leave when the lady of the house insisted that I clean the toilets. At that time, I quit babysitting permanently.

In 1974, I got married to a man who already had a 3-year-old son, and soon our daughter was born. While raising the kids, I tried welfare, unemployment, and eventually got a CETA job under then President Jimmy Carter's poverty program. I decided to abandon architecture and become a filmmaker. I taught myself sound recording by volunteering at a radio station. I learned cinematography and editing by observing other filmmakers. With some financial support from a lady at Newsreel, I made my first film, *Teach Our Children*, about the Attica Prison rebellion. Since then, I haven't stopped making movies—about 45 of them so far. My work does not really make money, though it has received quite a lot of recognition, especially, and surprisingly, from the mainstream media: an Academy Award nomination, Peabody, and Columbia du-Pont awards, to name a few. I got myself a steady

job teaching at a world-famous film school, New York University's Tisch School of the Arts, and so I'm able to pay my bills.

I am often asked why my films don't make much money, and the answer is, I think, because of their subject matter. They are not romantic comedies, nor Rambo-type action flicks filled with blood and sex. Instead, my films are generated from my personal experiences. I like to tell stories about society's underdogs: battered women, women in prisons, refugees, the dreams and nightmares of Asian-American immigrants, inter-ethnic conflicts, the HIV/AIDS epidemic, homeless people, miscarriages of justice, inadequate housing and child care, and the economic and political concerns of emerging countries in Africa, Latin America, and Asia. I believe outlaws should stick together and support each other. And I feel I'm able to capture these realities more honestly than our million-dollar, colorized, and manipulated national news media. My films get shown in theaters, on national television, and in classrooms, and in community centers, both in the United States and internationally. My films have an audience because my subjects have important things to say and unique contributions to make.

Today, I have relatively little power in the media world. I still struggle to get financial support, and it is still hard to finish a film. But I have succeeded in getting my thoughts and visual presentations out there. It is important that we as working women, women of color, women from the so-called Third World, mothers, daughters, and teachers help create a society where respect for human values is judged at least as positively as the chase for more dollar bills.

WHAT IS GOOD FOR NONTRADITIONAL EMPLOYEES IS GOOD FOR BUSINESS

SUMRU ERKUT, PhD

DESPITE nearly two decades of change, nontraditional employees continue to face barriers when moving up the corporate hierarchy. In the upper echelons of managerial positions, which lead to executive and CEO tracks, there is still just a handful of female, minority, new immigrant, and differently abled employees. Nontraditional employees have made inroads into upper management in support and staff functions such as human resources and legal affairs but they are still walled off from the high-opportunity tracks of the corporate world in the profit and loss centers, such as sales or manufacturing.

DIVERSITY AMONG EMPLOYEES

Businesses are confronted with a human-resource problem: In the coming decades women, minorities, recent immigrants, and the differently abled will replace the "traditional white male" employees as the majority of new entrants into the labor market. Because more and more nontraditional employees will be entering the work force, in comparison to the number of white men, it will be essential to promote more nontraditional employees to middle- and upper-management positions to replace the white men who reach retirement age.

Also, businesses will need to diversify their work force to remain competitive in a market place that includes growing numbers of women, minorities, immigrants, and differently abled consumers who have substantial buying power. In recent years, businesses have made voluntary agreements with minority leaders to hire more minority employees in order to protect their market share. For example, Coca-Cola USA promotes Hispanic-Americans to top management positions as part of its overall marketing strategy in the Hispanic community.

Still another motivating factor for businesses is to curb the recent exodus of talented women and minorities from corporate jobs. This trend has been attributed, in large part, to dissatisfaction with their mobility opportunities in traditional corporate hierarchies and to the inequities in compensation, especially for women.

GLASS BARRIERS

There is concrete evidence that nontraditional employees face glass ceilings in the corporate world. Women and minorities are consistently excluded from the upper rungs of corporate hierarchies, especially the corporate officer level. In the case of women, their representation among employees in executive, administrative, and managerial occupations has gone up from 26.5 percent in 1978 to 39.3 percent in 1988 to 41.5 percent in 1992. However, despite their growing presence among managers in general, women are estimated to hold *no more* than one to two percent of corporate officer positions at the top of the corporate hierarchy.

In the case of minority women, barriers to the upper rungs of the corporate ladder appear to be nearly impenetrable. A 1986 survey of women corporate officers found that the overwhelming majority of women respondents were white. Minority women made up only 3.3 percent of all women corporate officers who in turn made up no more than 2 percent of *all* corporate officers!

In addition to the glass ceilings, the existence of "glass walls" limits work options for nontraditional employees. For example, women are generally walled off from technical and engineering occupations. In 1992 women made up only 8.5 percent of engineers and 15.3 percent of architects. But in traditionally female occupations such as kindergarten and prekindergarten teachers, 98.6 percent of the workers are women. In addition, women are more likely to be promoted to management in occupations where there are already substantial numbers of women at lower levels. A survey in 1988 revealed that women were 48.9 percent of the executives, administrators, and managers in education and related fields, however, they held only 5 percent of the management positions in the field of construction inspectors.

WHAT BUSINESSES CAN DO

The following are recommendations that businesses can implement to address both their human resource problem and the glass barrier issue. The recommendations represent an array of options to improve the quality of work life for nontraditional employees. Because they have been formulated to improve the workplace, these recommendations will also benefit "traditional" employees who erroneously have been assumed to be a more homogenous group than they really are.

Promotion Policies. When promotions are based on informal criteria not fully spelled out or on criteria that are inconsistently applied, the result can be the promotion of people who are most similar to those making promotion decisions. This tendency limits nontraditional employees' opportunities for upward mobility. To avoid this pitfall, eliminate all criteria not integrally related to job performance and make promotion criteria objective and measurable. It is also essential to provide the necessary resources for newly promoted, nontraditional managers to insure that the promotion will be a success rather than a setup for failure. For example, many nontraditional employees complain that after a hard-won promotion, they find they are given budgets too small to do an effective job or they are left short staffed.

Career Development. High-risk, high-visibility, successfully completed assignments are often considered to be an important vehicle for corporate mobility. However, heading a start-up venture, handling international assignments, and troubleshooting may not be readily available to women and other nontraditional employees. In order to change this, business can encourage and reward managers to give high-risk, high-visibility assignments to nontraditional employees. In addition, business needs to provide training to upper-level managers on how to become effective mentors, including sensitivity training on cultural differences and recognition of sexual tensions.

Nontraditional employees can find training useful in learning how to pick a mentor and benefit from that relationship. Also, how to recognize and diffuse sexual tensions, and how to deal with racist, sexist, homophobic, or otherwise offensive comments and innuendoes.

Salary Equity. Compensation is a concrete, tangible indicator of one's worth. Existing evidence shows that women are underpaid and less satisfied with their pay. The National Commission on Working Women reported that in 1991 white, African-American, and Hispanic women were earning 68.7 percent, 61.9 percent, and 53.7 percent of white men's earnings, respectively.

Data on pay equity for the differently abled are also consistent with a pattern of inequity. At the national level, the annual earnings ratio of disabled to nondisabled male workers was 64 percent in 1987. The average disabled male worker earned $15,497 versus $24,095 earned by the average nondisabled male worker. The earnings ratio for disabled to nondisabled women workers was 62 percent in that same year. The average disabled female worker earned $8,075 versus $13,000 earned by the average nondisabled female worker.

In order to reach pay equity for nontraditional workers, businesses can ascertain that people doing the same job are paid the same regardless of gender, race, ethnicity, country of origin, or physical ability. Businesses can also apply principles of comparable worth to achieve equity in compensation so that people with comparable educational backgrounds, skills, and responsibilities are paid similar salaries.

Managing Diversity. Diversity in backgrounds, points of view, values, speech, and appearance can be a source of enrichment to the business. Too often, however, people who look or behave differently are highly scrutinized or ignored and undervalued, or they are tightly managed. Businesses can support diversity by communicating a clear policy about the organization's commitment to a diverse work force from the highest levels of the company. Tie this policy to measurable outcomes on which managers will be evaluated and rewarded. Managers must also be mindful that doubts and lower expectations can keep nontraditional employees outside the realm of good assignments, visible positions, and other opportunities to showcase their potential.

When any communication—written, oral, or visual—is being prepared, make it a policy to have it examined by nontraditional employees to detect and correct unintended biases or put-downs. Employees who are nontraditional in more than one way (e.g., being a minority female or a differently abled gay person), are often at double and even triple jeopardy for discrimination.

Improve Conditions at the Workplace. In subtle and not so subtle ways the physical and social environment can send messages about who is not valued, appreciated, and welcomed at work or expected to succeed. It is important to make the work environment fully accessible to the differently abled. Management also needs to send clear messages that sexist, racist, homophobic and otherwise offensive language, jokes, innuendo, posters, pictures, entertainment, etc., will not be tolerated. Make it official policy for all employees to attend "valuing differences" workshops, and provide frequent refresher courses.

Provisions for Handling Individual Grievances.
Offended employees often risk being labeled "trouble makers" if they complain of discrimination. There needs to be recourse for people who feel they have been unfairly treated. A company policy for hearing grievances and determining redress is essential. Businesses need to train their personnel to understand organizational dynamics so that, when an employee comes in with a problem, she or he will know how to separate work problems from personal problems. It is also helpful to establish an ombudsman's office where people who have work problems can talk about their concerns, get advice, find mediation services, realize redress, and get support without fear of reprisal.

Sensitivity training for offenders—people who knowingly or unknowingly act in ways that offend others—can be offered so they understand their offense, and it is hoped, stop the offensive behavior or business practice.

The solutions recommended here for businesses will improve working conditions for *all* employees. Changes such as these can bring out the best in each employee, especially nontraditional employees, who often feel unwelcome because the original designers of the modern management style did not consider the needs of nontraditional employees. When traditional management made rules for the workplace, they did not have women, minorities, immigrants, or the differently abled in mind. Nor did they have in mind that the traditional "corporate man" would also change, not only in response to social trends but also because each person's developmental needs change in the course of his or her adult life.

Today, with changing demographic trends, businesses cannot afford to ignore the different needs, wishes, tastes, values, orientations, and perspectives of nontraditional employees who will be making up the majority of new entrants into the work force in the year 2000. By focusing on the more obvious diversity that nontraditional employees present, businesses can become responsive to the diversity among all employees. The broad implication is that what is good for women and minorities is good for business because a responsive work environment is in tune with the changing needs, values, and choices of all of its employees.

Sumru Erkut is a senior research associate at the Center for Research on Women at Wellesley College where she conducts research on social policy-related issues. Her expertise is in women and minority issues and organizational cultures. Erkut also advises organizations and businesses facing the challenge of diversifying their work force.

Mable Thomas, 36, is a native Georgian and known to most Atlantans as "Able" Mable because of her political work. She was elected to the Georgia General Assembly in 1985 as its youngest member, and served for eight years before running for Congress.

I RAN FOR OFFICE in a low-to-moderate income area in Atlanta, and the power structure said that it would be impossible for me to get elected in this district as a grassroots candidate. first, they said, you don't have any money, and secondly, you cannot defeat a 19-year incumbent. Nevertheless, I was able to mobilize my community to launch successfully a grassroots movement to get me elected. The community elected me state representative by 71 percent of the vote.

It was about timing. Everything is about timing. It was time for people to be open to new leadership. You only have to be 18 years of age in order to work as a state representative. There's a mystique about politics that you have to be older, settled in your job, and know everybody. When Jesse Jackson ran for president, he dispelled those myths. He made people more accepting of the fact that I was a young person running. I was elected when I was 26 years old, becoming the youngest state representative in Georgia. At the time I was elected, I was also in my second term as vice president of the student government at Georgia State University and doing graduate work in public administration. I resigned my school office to devote more time to being a state repre-

sentative. Also at the time, I was Jesse Jackson's top delegate from Georgia to the Democratic National Convention.

Some of the obstacles I go through as a woman or as an African American are more subtle than overt. I can't just name a specific incident, but I look at the whole institution of Georgia. Ours is basically a conservative state. People in the Georgia Legislature are generally white, rural, males. A lot of them are property owners and their families have been involved in politics. They've been in power for a long time. Even though you might not be able to see racism overtly, it clearly exists in the Georgia Legislature. It goes through a seniority system and black people are just moving into it. It is hard to move through the system because you can't move faster than the seniority. When I was elected there were 21 black representatives out of 180 and six of those were women. And in the Georgia Senate, there were only six black men out of 56 senators.

The old boys' network is there and I'm not part of it. I'm not part of the back-room decisions, but it still comes down to one thing—they still had to deal with me because I had a vote. They had to come to me and ask my support on an issue, even though I was not part of the real decision making. I dealt with it as if everything was cool, but then I also took a principled position and didn't sell out regardless of whether or not my opinion was a popular one. In the whole system there are a lot of illusions of inclusion. But I'd rather know where I am at. And I'd rather have them deal with me because my principled position is in their face rather than for them to think I'm part of the good ol' boy system.

As the youngest state representative elected by the people without the power structure's blessings, I expected some resistance from the old guard leadership in the Georgia General Assembly. However, I had a very successful first term due to the fact that I refused to accept their negativity. I consistently worked to project a positive image. I spent my first year listening and building networks with fellow legislators. I was then able in the second year of my first term to author and pass three major pieces of legislation related to housing development and health care. Nationally, I am best known for landmark legislation that requires mammograms, pap smears, and prostate tests to be covered medical expenses. I was also responsible for a rape shield bill that states women's past sexual histories cannot be brought up in court during a rape trial.

After serving eight years I chose to run for Congress against a popular incumbent. Although I did not win the election, my career as a politician is far from over. I now own my own company, Master Communications, a leadership corporation whose sole purpose is to empower individuals and organizations to create and control their own unique vision. I am committed to transforming race relations in this country—to uplift and empower youth, and to create possibilities for integrity in our communities worldwide.

I feel very strongly about my faith in God, commitment to the people, and determination to improve the quality of life of Georgia's citizenry.

Rebecca Rangel, 42, specializes in self-esteem and empowerment for women, and cultural diversity awareness and appreciation for everyone. After obtaining two master's degrees and teaching university courses for seven years, Rangel decided to take a big risk and start her own business, Unlimited Woman Consultants.

I GREW UP in Fresno, California, with six brothers, a sister, and my mother. When I am asked what made me want to go to school and do the things I've done, it's hard to talk about it because a part of my growing up meant not dwelling on the difficulties. Instead, I take those hard times, learn from them, and move forward.

My mother raised all eight of us by herself. She is my *soul* source of inspiration and strength. When I was 12 she gave me an incredible amount of responsibility, like paying the gas and phone bill, and getting money orders for the rent. She always seemed to trust my judgment and made me feel like there wasn't anything I could not do. She is a rock of Gibraltar who often finds humor in the most desperate situations, and is highly intuitive to any disturbance going on with me. I find this to be a special kind of communication, especially since I live 160 miles from her.

From the age of 8, I have had a real curiosity for people and the ways in which they interact and treat each other. When I was about 18, I began noting the ways people treat each other according to their social, economic and oftentimes race. It became an obsessive interest for me.

I went to college for ten years, where sociology—the study of people and race relations—was always a part of my studies. It wasn't until my early twenties that I realized there was something wrong with how women were treated in society. I grew older and angrier at the same time, realizing that society indeed held a very real double standard for women.

I taught women and ethnic studies at San Jose State University and at two local community colleges as my primary work for seven years. I began working with adolescent Mexican-American women on their self-esteem in 1982, and realized that this was the work I loved the most. Since then, I have had several opportunities to work with women of diverse socio-economic and cultural backgrounds, teaching them self-esteem and personal empowerment. As a reaction to sparse teaching opportunities, I decided life was *entirely* too short to continue following the dollar sign and kissing people's feet. I do not remember ever being *so scared*, with the exclusion of the time my daughter disappeared from my side for two minutes in a department store! The thought of following academe felt like stagnation and suffocation. I had to do *something* that had *personal significance* for me.

I must acknowledge two influential factors: the Anita Hill/Clarence Thomas hearings in August 1991, and my daughter's birth in 1990. The hearings were a turning point in my life. I was convinced working to empower women to challenge old beliefs and barriers in their lives was my

Photo: Robin Stock

life's work. My daughter Jasmin's birth helped me realize that no matter how hard "a thing" seemed to be, I could no longer afford to stand back, hold back, or wait for someone else to do it. The Hindu expression, "Courage my friend, *you're it*, don't pretend you're not," states it best.

So in 1993 I began Unlimited Woman Consultants. Currently, I work at a middle school where the students are about 80 percent Hispanic. I teach self-esteem to two groups of young women. The gratification I receive is priceless. Basically, these young women are being trained to identify "the higher self within." Oh, I also get paid for this—it's the best of both worlds. I plan to take my company statewide, and eventually nationwide. That is daring to say, but I believe in myself.

I have spent the last year doing an enormous amount of soul searching, meditating, and cleaning house. Being an entrepreneur has forced me to become brutally honest with myself. Primarily out of need—spending time and energy on people and matters that deplete me have had to be eliminated. That was hard, but also one of the healthiest actions I've taken for myself ever! As women, we are conditioned to be caretakers, nurturers, supporters, and givers to others, seldom taking "selfish" action for ourselves. I have never felt more in tune with myself emotionally and psychologically. My work is about holding up a mirror to all women. Women are incredibly strong, and acknowledging that strength is one place to begin women's empowerment.

127

Jennifer L. Crandall, 35, owns her solo dental practice and dental building in San Francisco, which she independently started and financed.

NEARLY EVERYDAY I hear the question, "What made you want to be a dentist?" And, nearly every time I give an injection, my blood pressure takes a dash upward while I maintain an outward expression of ease and control for my patient. Often, during this time I'm thinking, "I wish this patient realized this event is more painful and stressful on my physical and psychological system than on hers." And then, I often wonder, "Why is it that I decided to do this?"

I'm the type of person who sets her mind to do something or to go somewhere, overcomes all obstacles to get it done and to be there. In high school I decided I would be a dentist. I could have a special skill no one could take away. I could have control of my time and my environment. Thus, it sounded like great freedom; I could go anywhere and use this skill to help others and I could choose where I wanted to live. Dentistry needs women doctors, and so does the public. Because of the demand and freedom, I made a beeline to become a dentist. I finished my college degree with three majors in three years and graduated from dental school and started my own practice from scratch at the age of 23.

In my approach to life I've always used obstacles as fuel for my life's engine. The obstacles or fuel that drove me down this career path were igniting: my mother telling me I'm crazy to want the headaches of my own business; my father telling me dental school is too expensive and he couldn't afford it (over $60,000 for three years of tuition alone in 1979); my college counselor telling me I'll never get accepted to dental school because I was too young, a female, and because I came from an unstable background of divorced parents. In dental school, instructors certainly tried to create their own barriers by keeping a severely critical eye on female academics and clinical performances. In addition I received sarcastic comments from lab instructors such as, "See ladies, it's just like baking a cake." Other obstacles included the practice-management instructors warning us about the problem of being too busy in dentistry, gloom and doom, and the impossibility of hanging a sign and starting a practice.

How did I hurdle? I presented to my college counselor six letters of acceptance from six of the seven dental schools I applied; a Bachelor of Arts with three majors in three years; and a Phi Beta Kappa. Being fortunate to have received one of seven scholastic and financial scholarships from the state of Arizona to a graduate program and with additional financial support from my mother, my father felt no burden. For the dental school clinical instructors, I made them scowl with envy because I made certain I experienced joy and had fun with my patients—enthusiastic properties that many instructors lacked. For the lab instructors who were grading my lab cases, I always asked

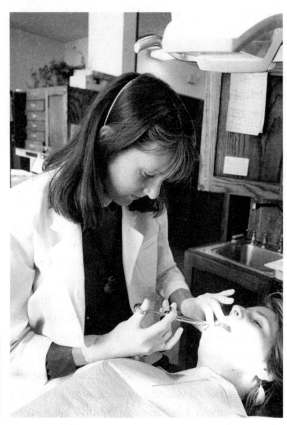

Photo: Nita Winter

other hats I must wear include employer, business person, collection person at times, lab person, janitor, receptionist, bill payer, and equipment service person. I also fall victim to insurance sales-people, financial planners, stockbrokers, and charitable organizations. At times, all these hats feel too tight and create tension headaches. But dentistry is dynamic and fun. It's arty, creative, and cosmetic with instant results. It's also extremely dynamic technologically. My work is challenging and demanding with new materials, equipment, and techniques constantly arriving. Being with different types of people all day long and sharing their life transitions and growth over six-month periods is inspiring. Most significantly, when I use my knowledge and skills to educate, diagnose, and ultimately heal is when my career feels most rewarding. I have a strong desire to help my patients understand their condition.

Having to numb someone is not fun and momentarily gives me second thoughts to what I'm doing in life. But, after thoroughly explain-ing, showing, and letting the patient participate in the dental care, I constantly get appreciation after the patient's treatment. I'm always delightfully surprised to get a "thank you." Everyone hates going to the dentist, and yet to get a "thank you," along with a referral, are the most wonderful compliments a dentist could ever receive; it's what keeps me going despite needles and noisy drills.

them if they liked chocolate-chip cookies as I batted my eyelashes, jokingly of course. The trick was not to take their offensiveness seriously. With respect to the doom and gloom practice manage-ment instructors, the key to success is truly to care. The success of developing a busy practice from one patient in an overly populated city of dentists such as San Francisco at 23 years old, and being able to own my own dental building by age 27, have been by-products of my sincere enthusi-asm and genuine care for my patients.

I love being a dentist, but Mom was right—owning a business can give one headaches. The

Natalie S. Gluck, 34, conducts research in optical thin-film physics at the Rockwell Science Center. Gluck is standing next to thin-film filter deposition chamber that she helped design and build.

I AM A SCIENTIST at the Rockwell Science Center, which is the corporate research center of a large, diversified company. My particular area of expertise is optical thin-film physics. In this research, we construct special kinds of mirrors and optical filters made by building up microscopically small layers of materials in unique arrangements. The physical principles involved are the same as those responsible for the colors that you see in oil slicks, soap bubbles, or even butterfly wings. A common example of a thin-film coating is found on iridescent sunglasses. However, we design, fabricate, and study much more complicated structures with unusual optical properties.

In my line of work, originality and independence are critical. I am a member of a team of scientists, each one expert in a particular aspect of our field. Although we routinely meet to discuss the status of our projects, I am expected to be self-reliant in deciding what research directions to pursue and how to overcome obstacles.

One of the things I enjoy most about my work is that I do a variety of different tasks. For example, one day I may develop or use computer programs to predict the optical behavior of a filter consisting of layers of materials in a specific arrangement. Later, I may use the apparatus I helped build to fabricate this filter and then use other equipment to measure its performance. Probably the most interesting part is when I find differences between the predictions and measured data. Then, my job is to explain the discrepancies and to identify a way around the problem.

Math and science are obviously crucial parts of my occupation, and they are areas that I very much enjoy. Unfortunately, I have seen how many women are discouraged from studying math and science. I experienced this type of prejudice in junior high and high school. For instance, in junior high, three quarters of the students in my advanced placement math class were girls, but by the time I took calculus five years later (my senior year of high school) I was the only girl left. The others had dropped out along the way because the teachers had discouraged them. I think I survived because I've always been stubborn and followed my interests regardless of what people thought. That's probably the main difference between me and the girls who dropped out; they were certainly smart enough to have done well in math if they had only tried and had been encouraged to continue.

I received a bachelor's degree in physics from the California Institute of Technology, and masters and PhD degrees in applied physics from Cornell University. Getting through Caltech was probably the most challenging experience in my career. The course work was very advanced and fast paced, and with so many bright fellow students it was hard to stand out. My experiences there taught me to do the best I could and not be afraid of making mistakes.

I think that the greatest impediment to becoming a scientist is to learn not to be intimidated by mathematics and science. In some ways, physics is like a foreign language, difficult to grasp at first but increasing the more you learn. Many women panic when they encounter difficulties, not realizing that everyone who attempts to learn has similar problems. A career in science is certainly a long-range endeavor, as it takes many years to progress through college, graduate school, and sometimes even postdoctoral experience. Try to remember, too, that what a scientist actually does after this long process is very much different from the basics encountered in school. I didn't finish school and start my first job until I was 27, even though I had followed a straightforward career path with no detours. I got married (to another scientist) when I was 29 and am only now expecting my first child at the age of 34. Nevertheless, I enjoy my work immensely and I think that the sacrifices I made along the way have been well worth the outcome.

A compromise that I and many other scientists have made is to direct our work towards more applied areas than those we studied in school. Economic and political trends have recently been very unkind to basic research. Companies such as the one I work for are far more demanding in their expectations of scientists today than they were in the past. They consider research to be an investment to benefit the company in the near future. Not all research is directed towards immediate needs, but certainly the emphasis now is strongly towards linking research to some potential payoff. Making research relevant to corporate goals is a delicate balancing act.

Photo: Winifred Meiser

Sandra Ann Taylor, 36, is head waitress at a deli-catessen. Taylor is in charge of hiring, scheduling, training, and making sure things run smoothly.

I WAS BORN and raised in New Jersey and I have always worked because it made me feel independent. For instance, I started working at the age of 8 shining doorknobs, so I never had to ask anybody for money and I felt the freedom of being what I pleased. I had many odd jobs after that.

After high school, I went into office work for about six years, but I got tired of sitting at a desk. On my lunch hour I went to a restaurant where my friend worked as a waitress. The place was always busy, so I helped her serve the food. I really loved it and thought it was fun because I am an energetic person. Of course, my friend thought I was crazy.

I decided to become a waitress. I picked my favorite restaurant and was determined to get a job there. I did, and ended up working there for three years. Then I moved to another city and started working in a delicatessen because it had a faster pace and I like it better than a dinner house. Another reason why I like waitressing is because I want to make people's meals more enjoyable.

Presently, I am the head waitress. This means I'm in charge of hiring, scheduling, training and making sure things run smoothly. Things don't always run smoothly though. People take their problems out on a waitress, but I really feel sorry for them—they don't even know how to control themselves. Also, when business is bad in a restaurant, it's always the waitresses' fault, but when business is good, they have nothing to do with it. And that's the truth.

But what really bothers me the most is that people sometimes have this attitude of, "Oh you poor thing you having to work on a Saturday night...." But this is the work I have chosen. That's why I carry myself the way I do. I take a lot of pride in myself and in my work, which is why I'm very good at what I do. Now I am taking classes in career development to help me discover what my next venture in the working world will be.

Photo: Beth Herzhaft

Gloria S. Riemenschneider, 60, and Jean Collins, 46, are certified nurse-midwives specializing in home births.

AT AN EARLY AGE, according to my mother, I talked of going into the mission field. I felt the call to serve God in the medical missions and graduated from Cornell University in 1949 with a Bachelor of Science in Nursing. When I found that I would be responsible for the obstetrical service in the small mission hospital to which I was assigned, I decided to study midwifery. In 1950, I graduated from the Maternity Center Association School of Nurse-Midwifery in New York City where my training was in home birth.

After being in Iran 19 years, I returned to work in the labor and delivery area of local hospitals. I found the change in obstetrical practice both awing and appalling. I was awed by the technological advances and their uses, but at the same time, appalled by their misuse. I decided to start a home-birth service when an anesthesiologist, upset by what he saw in hospital obstetrics, asked me to help him and his wife have a safe home birth. Researchers have shown that outcome in childbirth is not site related, but directly related to the health of the mother, prenatal care, competency of the birth attendants, and appropriate use of technology. Many well-educated women have chosen what, throughout history, has been the normal site for birth and remains so in much of the world today—the home.

At this point, midwives and obstetricians are polarized, but it really need not be so. Obstetrical as well as family practice specialists have much to offer the midwives and the midwives have much to offer the specialists. The practices really complement one another. A close-working relationship between them would certainly improve obstetrical care and outcome. Midwives and doctors in many countries have a close-working, collaborative relationship no matter where the site of service. Why can't this be true in the United States where freedom of choice is one of our basic rights? According to the philosophy of the American College of Nurse-Midwives, every childbearing family has a right to a safe, satisfying experience with respect for human dignity and worth; for variety in cultural forms; and for the parents' right to self-determination.

Gloria

I NEVER KNEW what I wanted to be. Remote relatives asked and expected an answer. But at school's end and at the age of 17, I still did not have one. It did not take many days behind a desk for me to decide that wasn't for me, so on my 18th birthday I became a student nurse. In England, it is customary for qualified nurses (who are called state registered nurses) to continue their education and specialize in a field of their choice. I chose midwifery and have not regretted my choice.

I landed in the "New World" in 1962. I felt I had taken a step back in time after leaving a country that helped women have babies in their own homes amongst their loved ones. I found myself "helping" women by giving them IV injections of scopolamine and restraining them in their beds with side rails and sometimes strapping their hands down. These women would deliver, and maybe two hours later, see their baby. Since then, we have come full cycle. Yes, now we truly help mothers have their babies together with family, alert, participating in the birth experience, encouraging involvement and preparation. We can do more. Many expectant mothers are not aware of the services available through certified nurse-midwives and the dedicated care and educational experience they offer as an alternative way to have a baby, which is a natural process.

Being a nurse-midwife in America means to be always fighting. Fighting for the right to assist parents in a natural process, because some in the medical profession want to make it an unnatural process and invade the maternal body and fetus for tests and procedures. Fighting to stay in the profession without feeling that every day may be your last because an insurance company cannot be found willing to back nurse-midwives as liability coverage.

Midwifery is a profession of extreme emotions. It is working with women and their families to guide them, encourage them, and initiate them in the intricacies of childbirth. It is my wish for every pregnant woman I come in contact with to have the most joyous, wonderful obstetrical experience possible. The disappointment in this profession is that obviously, not everyone meets this goal.

Jean

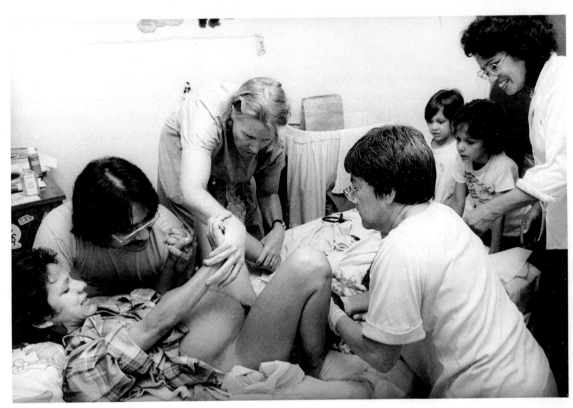

Photo : Martha Tabor

Melanie R. Bond, 42, is a zoo keeper specializing in the care of gorillas and orangutans. Bond has worked with small mammals, reptiles, and primates at the Smithsonian's National Zoo for 20 years.

ONE OF MY FIRST BOOKS was *Zippy the Chimp's Birthday Party*, perhaps that shaped my future career! From an early age I liked animals. I considered veterinary school, but decided I didn't want to be around animals in pain. On graduation from college, my dad encouraged me to apply for a keeper job at the National Zoo where he had often taken our family when I was a child. I was one of the first women hired at the Smithsonian's National Zoo in 1973, although European zoos have a long tradition of female keepers. Some co-workers believed that someone who was a college graduate would not be happy cleaning up after animals. Some thought women would be physically and emotionally unsuited to the work. A few gentlemen at first refused to allow "us girls" to carry hay bales or feed sacks. But after pointing out that we were paid the same wage to do the same work and that we would ask for help if needed, we soon reached a cordial compromise.

I have worked with small mammals, reptiles, and primates, from the tiny, highly endangered golden lion tamarin to the largest of the great apes, the gorilla, and its Asian cousin, the orangutan. I've been working with apes since 1975 and there's no place in the zoo I'd rather be. Apes are intelligent, powerful, emotional beings. It never ceases to amaze me that they can be so human one moment, and so totally nonhuman the next. But they are never *inhumane* or *mock* human, as so often portrayed in the media. I feel we have helped change the public's view through education about real apes and their plight in the wild, even though most people come to the zoo primarily to be entertained.

I care for eight gorillas and nine orangutans, plus some monkeys and gibbons, a job I share with several other keepers in the Primate Unit. Most of our time is spent cleaning enclosures, preparing diets, and feeding the primates. We also notify the veterinarians if we suspect one of our charges is sick or injured, and assist in examinations, treatment, and medication. Finding ways of constructively occupying the time of these curious yet powerful animals is a continuous challenge. They have a short-attention span and are easily bored, but are so strong they demolish children's toys in just a few seconds. We also talk with visitors, families, and school groups about these animals and their wild relations.

Some of our apes can use a few signs of American Sign Language, but they all understand spoken English much better than pet dogs and cats. The orangutans understand "show me your hurt," and let me medicate them or examine injuries with the veterinarians. This communication has encouraged an even closer bond between me and my "red-haired friends," and has allowed me such privileges as a mother placing her new-

Photo: Martha Tabor

born in my hands!

Orangutans and gorillas live more than 50 years in a zoo. One of the greatest things about my job is being able to keep them healthy, happy and safe, and to watch them grow and develop from helpless infants to handsome adults. Building a relationship of mutual trust and affection with entire families of these wonderful beings is a feeling that can't be put into words, but can be seen and appreciated by thousands of zoo visitors.

Now I can contribute to the well-being of many more animals since being appointed as administrator of the stud book for orangutans in North America. I had to acquire new computer skills in order to keep track of orangutan births, deaths, and moves from one zoo to another. I traveled to Indonesia to attend an international conference on great apes. I meet regularly with other zoologists to coordinate efforts to preserve this species in zoos and in the wild.

The best kind of job satisfaction comes at the end of the day when the last meal is fed, and I can spend five minutes of quiet time with Indah, a 13-year-old orangutan. For years we have done this together. I marvel that I have spent almost 20 years learning about these fascinating beings, and realize that there is still so much to know!

Deborah Glockner-Ferrari, 43, is president and co-founder of the nonprofit organization Center for Whale Studies. She is a pioneer in the underwater study of the humpback whale, a critically endangered species, and one of ten scientists appointed to the US Humpback Whale National Recovery Team. Initially, Glockner-Ferrari worked nights as a waitress to support her daytime research, and in the off season, an assortment of jobs.

FROM ATOP the ocean's surface, I peered through my mask into the depths below. About 50 feet beneath me, a humpback whale mother and calf lay motionless. Excitedly, I photographed their greyish-black flippers and the calf's tiny white chin and mottled belly. Gradually, the calf began to rise. As it approached within several feet of my camera, I quickly counted the lip grooves below its mouth. They numbered three. I had previously found that the lip groove pattern could be used to identify each whale, the pattern being unique to the individual, much like human fingerprints. I then noted that the young calf was a female. With her eyes opened wide, she watched me as I observed her. The calf appeared to be very curious. She spouted three times at the surface, swimming in a small clockwise circle. Then, she sounded, diving down towards her mother.

Several minutes passed by. The mother and calf rose together, spouting in unison. The calf playfully twirled her body and began to swim upside down. Her eyes were now closed. The mother gently touched her calf with her flippers. Slowly, they descended into the depths below. A feeling of peacefulness pervaded the waters.

To the beauty of nature itself and to my absolutely wonderful parents, I owe my love of whales and dolphins. Born in New Orleans, I grew up in Louisiana in a beautiful little town of Covington nestled in a forest along the winding Bogue Falaya and Tchefuncte rivers. As for my education, I graduated in 1972 from Louisiana State University with a Bachelor of Science degree in biochemistry. After working in this field for a while, I began practicing transcendental meditation (TM). As TM became an integral part of my life, my heart opened even more to seeing the beauty of wildlife and all of nature. I obtained a summer job at an oceanarium in Gulfport,

Photo: Mark Ferrari

Photo: Mark Ferrari

Mississippi, as a dolphin trainer, followed by a lab assistant position at the University of Hawaii dolphin lab. In 1975, I had my first opportunity to observe a humpback whale mother and calf underwater. I knew then that I wanted to study whales and dolphins in their natural environment as my lifetime work.

I began an annual study of humpback whales in the waters off the west coast of Maui, Hawaii. Using benign photographic techniques, I identified individual whales, focusing on mothers and calves by photographing the color pattern on their bodies, the numerical pattern of their lip grooves, the shape of the dorsal fin, and any unusual scarring. Using a 15½-foot inflatable Zodiac to slowly motor to an area in which whales are located, I'd gently enter the water with only snorkeling equipment and camera gear to make underwater observations and identifications. In 1979, I discovered a simple technique to determine the sex of a whale by observing the lateral view of the whale for the presence of a lobe found only in females. I soon found that I was able to track individual whales of known sex over successive years. Through identifying known mothers and calves over successive years, I was able to determine that some females had an unexpectedly high reproductive rate and were capable of producing calves annually.

In 1980 my husband, Mark Ferrari, a sensitive, and talented wildlife photographer and cinematographer, joined the project. Together we continued the study and discovered that the percentage of humpback whale mothers and calves resting in near-shore waters was decreasing dramatically each year as high-speed, near-shore "thrillcraft" activities were increasing and water quality decreasing. We worked to have the state of Hawaii pass legislation that banned the use of thrillcraft in Maui during the whale season.

Using a 19½-foot cuddy cabin boat to conduct our ocean work, we are now celebrating our 20th field study observing humpback whales. We have taken over 120,000 photographs identifying approximately 1,500 individual whales, while recording their behavior, and determining essential facts about the reproductive cycle and vital parameters of the whale population. We are also currently participating in the development of a management plan for a Humpback Whale Sanctuary that has been designated for Hawaiian waters.

In 1990, our little girl was born and she immediately became an integral part of our team. Now 4 years old, Chantelle helps search for whales and actively participates in collecting and preserving skin samples that have been sloughed by individually known whales. We later send these skin samples to Cambridge University for DNA fingerprinting and genetic analysis. The most wonderful gift of my life is to have been given a little one with whom I can share my experiences. It is my greatest joy to share with her the beauty of whales and of all life. For Chantelle and for all the children of the world, I hope to continue our long-term study of the humpback whale and to contribute to the conservation of this endangered species and the environment we all share.

JoAnn Soge Track, 35, is a Native-American potter. Track traveled internationally before returning to her home and continuing the tradition of her grandmother, working in the pueblo's well-known mica clay.

I FEEL THAT I have always had a choice as to where I want to be and what it is that I want to be doing. After graduation from high school, I attended the Institute of American Indian Arts where I studied writing, ceramics, theater, and modern dance. After one-and-a-half years in Santa Fe, I very much wanted to travel, so I went to New York City, then on to Paris for the summer. The Louvre was fascinating, and I was astonished by the private collections of native art. While in France I traveled and saw as much as I could.

After the summer, I returned to New York City and stayed with friends. While in the city I met a lot of Latinos. We talked about our lives and the struggle of native people. In 1971, I went to Cuba to help fidel Castro in the sugar-cane harvest. After two months of hard work and studies on Marxist/Leninist theory and socialism, I decided to return to New York City, and then to my home, Taos Pueblo. Not being able to find a job, I went to the Navajo reservation and attended Navajo Community College. After two years, I returned to Taos Pueblo.

After being away for some time, I realize the importance of our ancient styles, although I also have to allow my own creative needs to influence my work. I come from a family of artists, so I can't help but be inspired to work with the native clay from which we all come. My grandmother taught me how to respect our special clay and how to allow my spirit to emerge in the form of pottery. My grandmother worked in our pueblo's well-known mica clay. I am proud to carry on for my generation.

Photo: Scott Fields

JoAnn Falletta, 39, is the music director and conductor of the Virginia Symphony and the Long Beach Symphony. Falletta also works with the Women's Philharmonic in San Francisco.

MY MUSIC STUDIES began when I was 7 years old. I played guitar, piano, and cello. About the time I was 12, my parents started taking me to concerts and I fell in love with the orchestra. I never had experienced anything like that, seeing a group of people working together to create something so special. It was then that I decided I wanted to be able to shape the interpretation of that magnificent instrument, the symphony orchestra.

I first went to the conservatory at the age of 18. I spent an entire year before I was permitted to major in conducting because the college administrators said that no woman had ever had success in the field. They didn't want to encourage me to be a conductor because they could not envision any chance of my success in that exclusively male domain. It took me a year to convince them. Their resistance surprised me. I just kept doing as well as I could in my courses and telling them that I was interested and I recognized that it had never been done. I was lucky when a new teacher came to the school who was a little younger and more understanding about the possibilities for women.

Today, there remain some reservations to a young American woman conductor on the part of the major symphonies, particularly the older musicians and older board members. We will change that attitude through professionalism and hard work. Sometimes it is more of a professional challenge to be an American musician. On the highest levels of music making in the United States, we are very prejudiced against home-grown talent. There is often a preference given to European conductors because they come from a different cultural background than our own. I think it's an American inferiority complex that we've always emulated Europe, and this can be frustrating for American artists.

For the last few years I have been extremely busy. I have three orchestras and I conduct about 120 concerts a year. I could never have predicted this ten years ago. I had the good fortune to be invited as a guest conductor all over the United States, Europe and Asia. When I was just starting out, there were times when I was very depressed; I knew my parents always wanted me to go to law school. As little as ten years ago they'd say, "Why not think about law school?" Conducting is such an unstable career. I never knew if it was going to work for me. But I always felt that somehow I would make it because I knew I wanted it so much.

I feel that it is a tremendous privilege to be working as a musician in the United States. There is potential, a desire, an openness to new ideas that is challenging and stimulating. Of course, there are disappointments and difficulties, but the moments of magic more than make up for them.

Photo: Nita Winter

To hear a Mozart symphony take shape in your hands, to see an orchestra work with all its heart and talent towards the creation of something beautiful, to feel that together we have moved and uplifted our audience beyond the cares and troubles of their everyday lives—all this makes working as a conductor the realization of my most cherished dream. One doesn't choose music, music chooses you—and fills your life with pain, frustration, loneliness, insecurity, passion, turmoil, happiness, grief, anxiety, intensity, peace, satisfaction, dissatisfaction, longing, desire, hard work, and the most incredible joy I could ever imagine.

Penelope "Penny" Bishonden, 49, cares for lions and tigers on a private, nonprofit game reserve called Shambala where she lives, tending to the lions' needs on a 24-hour basis. Shambala is part of the Roar Foundation, which was founded by the actress Tippi Hedren.

I HAVE HAD a lifelong preoccupation with cats; from my beloved nanny's tabbies when I was barely 2; wanting to comfort the sad old lion in the early Los Angeles Zoo; my essays in school on cats; drawing them; bringing home strays; and making my own conclusions as to why the lions didn't eat Daniel. These early aspects led to painting lions to support my young sons and exhibiting in wildlife benefit art shows. If someone had ever asked me what I wanted, my answer would have been "a lion."

The years I've spent with these cats have been an intensely personal experience, perhaps because my personality, genetic heritage, and childhood set me up for it. Love is not enough for the job, since it requires your whole attention, and at least for me, first place in my life. My success in caring for the lions has not brought financial rewards, but rather gifts of the spirit and an absolute belief in the holiness of nature and animals.

I had at one time entertained the idea of becoming a vet, thinking that short of moving to Africa, this was my only hope of working near them. I had completed most of the -ologies and -atomies—micro, bio, etc.—but marriage and two sons moved hope of more college into the area of maybe.

However, visions do come true. I first met Tippi Hedren 21 years ago, and she was carrying a lion cub. None of my experiences would have been possible without Tippi Hedren (who starred in *The Birds* movie, and others). She gave me the opportunity and autonomy, and provided all the support systems and large compounds necessary to allow as near a natural life as a captive lion, tiger, leopard, and cougar might know. I work with three women who are cat handler-trainers, and a couple of men who also work as handler-trainers. Sadly, many men are too harsh with the cats and do not care to take instruction from women. Here at Shambala we only want to nurture and support the cats, not show off.

In the beginning, caring for the lions was a very "bootstrap operation." It called on my information-seeking ability to learn how to sustain life in tiny newborn cubs whose captive mothers wouldn't feed them. Sometimes I had to take over as surrogate mother and bottle feed cubs taken from their mothers at about 4 weeks old. The surge of love and protectiveness I felt upon holding my first cub shook me to the core and the feelings have only grown with the years. It was exactly as though I had given birth to them. I love them more now at 500 pounds than I did at their birth weight of 3 pounds. My handling of animals has not won me any popularity contests with some of the other people with whom I've worked. I am sure I have been a great inconve-

nience at times since my methods are based on patience and doing it the lion's way. Never once has a male employee asked how I do what I do.

I never wanted to be a trainer in the commonly accepted definition (male definition) in films or commercials because I felt this was exploitive and perpetuated all the folklore myths and misconceptions about big cats. I also felt the methods were cruel. The life most working big cats live is deplorable, with no attention given to their instinctual needs. They are put to death, or worse, they are auctioned off to circus-breeding farms or canned hunts when they are no longer a financial gain to their owners. Through the years I have modified these beliefs somewhat. There are a few trainers who truly love their animals, but who were taught by the good ol' boys' network of trainers. When they saw how well we treat our cats, they were eager to change.

Whatever it takes, I will do my part to help wild animals survive. I feel that the three factors that contribute to the demise of wild animals on this planet are human overpopulation, chemical pollution, and exploitation by humans as objects of entertainment and financial gain. If we continue to mishandle the byproducts of our civilization such as radioactive waste and unchecked real estate development, there will be no open land left for human beings, let alone animals. The voice of the lion and whale are inseparable parts of human racial memory. When they die, we die. I believe the Great Spirit gave us this earth to cherish and everything we do for wild animals counts. I simply want to do what's right while there's still a chance.

One does not "dabble" in lions. I don't know all the answers and if someone can prove to me a way to improve things for big cats, I'll change yesterday. I truly hope I can assist others with what I've learned. The one thing I want to see as I leave this lifetime is the face of a lion, and I promise you I'm not coming back unless children in 200 years and beyond can dream of a life such as mine. They deserve to see wildlife as it was meant to be...not taxidermy displays in museums or as trophy heads hanging over mantelpieces.

Barbara Howard Black, 28, has been a secretary since she was 18 years old.

I HAVE WORKED for ten years in the government, even working before I finished high school. Office work is a pleasure. Experience has ripened me for just about any situation. I can work steadily for hours before realizing that I am hurting my back and eyes by the position and lighting of the work station.

I take pleasure in being able to make a readable object out of a rough draft pasted together. Deciphering work that's hard to read is difficult, and then people want it back right away. I've got to do perfect work, do it on time, and be happy—all at the same time. Usually what happens is on a Friday they'll give me a big mess and say, "It's due today." Then they leave. So, I have burning eyes and a headache, but it's got to be perfect. Then on Monday, it'll be all ready, and they'll change it all around and say, "Get this ready by 10 o'clock." And then I'm told, "You really do good work." About then, I'm leaning forward, ready to hear some more praise, and that's it. That's all.

I don't get much training on the office machines, mostly it's trial and error. Sometimes I wipe out the whole thing on the computer. But I like teaching others. It's good to be able to teach and see the results—to see how that person learns. My supervisor told me, "You're too good." I feel even better that I have learned to master a few office machines in the process. I feel like an expert when it comes to some computer work, but in this day and age, I have to educate myself continually to keep abreast of growing office automation and changes.

I have two children, ages 6 and 2, and they are what's behind my working. If I don't care for them, who will? Public assistance and food stamps are just surviving. If I didn't have the children, sometimes I think I wouldn't be working—just be a bag lady or a street person. I've been legally separated from my husband for three years. Sometimes he wants to get back together, but I won't do that to myself or my kids.

Through it all, my neck still cramps when I sit still and type too long. But I love typing.

Photo: Martha Tabor

Barbara Ann Shore, 34, is an ordained Presbyterian minister and psychologist, working as a psychiatric chaplain. Raised in a nonreligious family that did not encourage a college education, Shore considers this an unlikely profession given her background.

WORKING as a member of an acute treatment team with mentally ill patients is undeniably both discouraging and stimulating. I work with a physician, nurse, social worker, and psychological examiner to offer the best possible care for the people we treat. Political, legal, cultural, institutional, and familial intricacies often seem to thwart effective interventions. Yet, I am convinced that even one person can make a difference in the midst of all these complications and obstacles. One person trying to figure out what it will take to create or instigate change, trying to help what at times appears to be a hopeless situation…trying to stop what often seems to be an endless destructive cycle.

Raised in a nonprofessional and nonreligious family, perhaps I am not the most likely person to become an ordained minister and psychologist. My family did not encourage higher education, and I am the only one in the family to have attended college and graduate school. My parents' views were traditional; women were above all expected to marry. When I entered graduate school, I had no idea as to the amount of prejudice and discrimination I would encounter. Despite the fact that I entered the second-largest seminary in the United States, there was no female faculty teaching required courses. A number of the male faculty were quite vocal about their assumptions that the few women in the seminary were there only because they were "man hunting" or because sexual favors had "earned" them a spot. The prejudice and discrimination within the church has been rampant, and for the most part unchanging. What has changed is that the individuals in power are simply less likely to vocalize their feelings quite as freely. This, regretfully, only makes sexism more difficult to manage. Therefore our problems continue. Although women have been ordained in the Presbyterian Church for over 50 years, there is a shamefully small percentage of women ordained. I currently reside in a presbytery that still has never ordained a woman.

Understandably, my initial experiences in the ministry were marked by the fact that above all I was female—for better or for worse. On the one hand it meant continued discrimination, even to the point of job loss when trying to confront sexual harassment, and on the other hand, it meant opportunity. Women literally flocked to me for pastoral counseling. Perhaps this should not have surprised me given that one out of every four women (and maybe even higher) is thought to have been physically or sexually abused or raped during her lifetime. These statistics are thought to be even higher within religiously oriented families. Further recent research suggests that between 70 and 80 percent of all persons seeking counsel-

Photo: Callie Shell

my anger over the world's injustices. It took my fears over meaninglessness. It took determination which some might label as a form of stupidity in my case. It took serendipity, often literally, in the form of miracles. It took a sense of mystery. And above all, it took a fundamental belief in the worth of all persons. What were the costs? In the most concrete sense, they were far more than I fear I will ever be able to compensate for. Despite working the entire time I have been in school, I owe thousands of dollars in school loans. I do not own a house, a couch, or even a bed. I drive a 20-year-old car that is broken nearly as often as it runs. More importantly however, were the personal costs. I have never married, and I fear that I may lose the opportunity ever to experience pregnancy and birth. I have been separated from my friends and family for years, although I have had the delightful privilege of making many new friends.

Limited acceptance has come all too slowly and the barriers are encountered daily. Despite ten years in the ministry, I have only had the opportunity of hearing one other woman preach. But the networking grows slowly, as does the opportunity to encourage and support others and to develop uniquely as a female minister. We have distinctive gifts to offer as women, ones that I cannot help but believe will forever change and enhance ministry as we know it today.

ing go to a minister, rabbi, or other religious professional, rather than to a psychologist, psychiatrist, or other licensed mental-health professional. This would not be a problem except that the majority of religious professionals have no, or at best minimal, psychological training.

So how did I get to be where I am today? It took the support and kindness of friends, even when they didn't agree with my individual decisions. It took the wisdom of others when I came and told them that I was not so slowly going insane. It took the generosity of others when I didn't have two nickels to rub together. It took

Cecilia Kienast, 58, has been a deputy sheriff for the past 28 years. For the last 20 years she has been assigned as a supervisor and detective sergeant in the homicide bureau.

I HAVE WORKED as a deputy sheriff in the largest sheriff's department in the world in one of the largest counties in the country. The journey took me through the police academy, the women's jail division, narcotics bureau as an undercover agent-investigator, juvenile bureau, detective division, and a lengthy assignment in the homicide bureau.

All new deputies on my department are assigned to work in the supervision of inmates in custody. In the 1960s, women were kept in such assignments for as long as ten years as there were few positions for women in mainstream law enforcement. Within a year I was presented with the opportunity to be assigned to the narcotics bureau. Having this opportunity after only one year as a deputy placed me in the position of having to risk change in order to grow. That first choice, to be willing to leave a secure, traditional women's assignment, to work in a bureau of 60 male law enforcement officers, and to become the only woman officer assigned to that bureau, was the most difficult choice of my career. That choice taught me to risk and walk through the fear. Once I had accepted the assignment, the doors of opportunity were opened to me and lead to my eventual assignment and lengthy stay

as the first woman in the homicide bureau.

The work was challenging, interesting, and seldom boring. The difficult part was not in the problem-solving nature of our work as much as the stress involved with the grief suffered by humanity. The women of my era in law enforcement were caught in the midst of great social change as the job moved from nontraditional for women to "almost" traditional. We were exposed to many different attitudes from the men with whom we worked. These attitudes varied from open-minded, all-encompassing acceptance to utter contempt. We were also exposed to many practices that were biased against women at one end of the spectrum and protective of women at the other end. The exposure to these attitudes has developed within me a strong sense of being centered, which is based in self-knowledge and self-respect as opposed to an "other-directed" need for approval. I thank the men in law enforcement who presented the challenge and the painful experiences that led me to this place.

Each job experience is altered by an individual's perception and I believe it is this individuality that takes a work situation and transcends it into a personal contribution to society. Law enforcement is one of those careers that demands from us a strong personal commitment to seek truth and to help others, therefore, such a career is indeed noble. The journey has been challenging, interesting, heartbreaking, and oftentimes, devastating.

I marvel at the growth of a young woman and mother who began her law enforcement career as

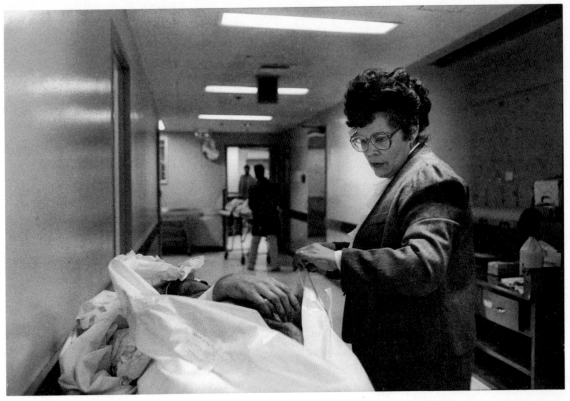

Photo: Gary McCarthy

a very sensitive and quiet soul who has evolved into a mature and confident woman—a woman who can tenaciously pursue and arrest a violent offender, understanding the circumstances which may have led him to his deeds, but sees the greater need to protect the general welfare of society.

It has been especially rewarding to have pursued this journey and remained sensitive to the sorrow of victims, the pain of parents whose children are troubled, injured, murdered or missing, and the devastation of people's dreams. This sensitivity allowed me to share in the pain, sorrow, and sometimes joy of the people with whom I came

in contact. It is an "amazing grace" to be so fortunate in a career thought to be a "man's world," to have come full circle in that career knowing that I brought to law enforcement many "womanly gifts" to share with humanity.

Throughout the course of my career my family remained the most important aspect of my life. My husband was there for me throughout the many years of long hours, stressful cases, and difficult decisions. Our daughters are women who have made positive choices and who have added to our lives wonderful grandchildren. I have surely been blessed in my life and my work.

Elizabeth Shanov, 40, is a sports journalist, covering Los Angeles area sports for ABC Radio Network. Coverage of major events include the 1984 Summer Olympics, Super Bowls, World Series, NBA Championships, home games for all the city's major sports teams, and more. She began her broadcasting career in 1975.

ASSIGNMENT: Cover the NBA basketball game between the Los Angeles Lakers and the Utah Jazz at the Forum, Inglewood, California.

6:30 P.M.: Arrive at Forum. Call the night producer in New York. "OK, I got it. You want interviews with two people from the winning team, one from the losing team. Let's hope for a fast game." Deadline: 10 p.m., Pacific time. The show goes on the air at 10:09 p.m.

7:38: Game starts.

7:50: This is going to be a blowout. The Lakers already have a huge lead.

8:05: Uh-oh, trouble. A Utah player is hurt. Game delayed. This deadline is definitely in jeopardy.

9:15: Lakers lead by 30 points. Pray for no fouls… fouls stop the clock and drag out the game.

9:38: Game ends. The coaches can keep the locker room closed to reporters for no more than ten minutes (NBA rules). Meeting the deadline is still possible.

9:40: Interview Jazz coach. A real stand-up comedian. He uses several obscenities in answering the question. It'll make a good tape for the "never-used-for broadcast blooper reel," but right now Liz needs clean language, and a pithy quote for the show. She gets it.

9:48: Rush into Laker locker room. Talk to head coach who comes up with a good quote quickly. More interviews with players.

9:58: A mad dash to the pressroom telephone. Tape rewinding as she runs. Liz remembers the exact answers from each of the players that she will send to the producer in New York. As she rewinds the tape, she notes the positions of those answers.

9:59: Connect the tape recorder to the phone with alligator clips. Connect the microphone into the tape recorder.

10:00: Call the producer. Relay names of the interviewees, how many points they scored, any pertinent facts about the quotes, and transmit the tape. Liz makes the deadline.

"**WOW!** You mean you get to go into the *locker rooms?*" That's always the first thing they want to know when they find out I'm a sports reporter. Well, yes, professional sports teams in the United States finally agreed in the 1980s that a female sports reporter deserves the same access to the players and coaches that a male reporter has. So, yes, I do get to go into locker rooms. But people who think that a post-game interview in a sweaty, smelly, crowded clubhouse is a glamorous or titillating experience…well, they've never been there.

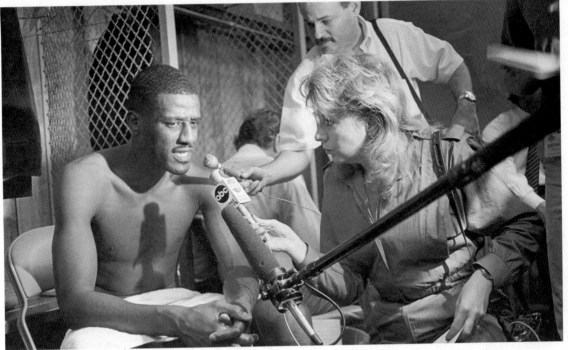

Photo: Walt Mancini

Actually, most players will either stay in their uniforms or wear towels during an interview. Sure, there are a few who try to embarrass or shock women reporters by strutting around stark naked. It has changed since the ugly incident involving Lisa Olson in Boston in which football players exposed themselves to her and verbally assaulted her. Olson sued the club, and since then the teams themselves have cracked down on such exhibitionism. And most '90s athletes have dealt with female reporters on their way up, in high school, college and the minor leagues. They're not as surprised to see women in the locker rooms as their counterparts were ten years ago.

Frankly, in the '90s, women reporters sometimes have more problems with insecure, jealous male colleagues than they do with athletes. The "old boys' club" does a great job in back stabbing and character assassination against good, aggressive female journalists. The stuff being slung at Hillary Rodham Clinton is old hat to us. You've got to realize that the problem is theirs, not ours...but that's hard to do when it costs you a job.

I'm glad to be working in Los Angeles. Women sports reporters are an accepted fact of life at most media outlets here. There are female sportswriters, television camera operators, photographers, and broadcasters. We've all been hit by flying athletic supporters (underwear, not fans) and called every sexist term for "woman" that's ever appeared in *Playboy*. But when I was doused by champagne in a victory celebration...well, that's when I knew the players had decided, "She's OK. She belongs."

Clarita Berroga Suniga, 35, has been working in sugar-cane fields for the past 12 years. Originally from the Philippines, she moved to Hawaii with her husband in 1971, and they have three children. Suniga spoke about her life and work in a conversation.

WHEN I CAME to Hawaii, I could speak only a little English. I learned by hearing, but not that much. My children help me, they correct my English. I didn't go to college, not even high school…I only go to the sixth grade in the Philippines. After that, I worked on the farm with my parents. I grow rice, corn, tomatoes, eggplant, and I sell these things at the market.

I had to find money, that's why I left the Philippines. In Hawaii, I worked at a pineapple cannery, but not too long, about six months, then they closed the company. I got a job at a plantation and they showed me how to work in the fields. I start work at 7 in the morning and work until 3:30; I cut the cane and lay it out. A tempered knife cuts the cane real easy, but my hands get tired from cutting the cane all day, and sometimes they get numb. I rub them with alcohol, that helps.

I like the job, it's not so hard. The only thing, it's hot and makes me tired. I wear coveralls and long sleeves.

I make $7.31 an hour, and 12 years ago I got $4 an hour. My husband works for the same company as a truck driver. Now, we have a house in Lihue and we have a car. My children, I tell them to study more so they don't do work like I do. I want them to go to college.

Photo: Ann Meredith

SEXUAL HARASSMENT: *What It Is, What to Do About It*

COLLEEN PHELAN

AS WOMEN preparing for the world of work, we explore our career options, develop new skills, undertake internships, and other on-the-job experiences. We believe our talents and hard work will be recognized and rewarded. We expect to be treated fairly and with respect by our supervisors and co-workers. And in many ways we will be. Yet, experts estimate that approximately 50 to 75 percent of American women will experience some form of sexual harassment during their academic and work lives. While sexual harassment is not an aspect of the workplace most women anticipate, being prepared to address harassment is essential to every woman's career planning. The keys to preparing for this workplace hazard are understanding what sexual harassment is, how it can affect a woman and her work, and what to do if it happens.

The first step toward being prepared to address sexual harassment is understanding what it is. Harassment in general means to bother someone with unwelcome attention. Sexual harassment is to bother someone in a sexual way. This unwanted sexual attention can be as blatant as a forced kiss and as subtle as a comment about someone's appearance. Sexual harassment can be in the form of spoken words, touches, stares, whistles, catcalls, gestures, and displays of graphic materials. When this behavior takes place in the workplace, it is illegal. Sexual harassment is a violation of Title VII of the 1964 Civil Rights Act, which protects women and others from employment discrimination.

There are two basic forms of sexual harassment: *quid pro quo* (Latin for "one thing in return for another") and hostile environment. In the first type, *quid pro quo*, a supervisor makes unwelcome sexual advances and either states or implies that the employee must submit in order to keep her job or receive a promotion or raise. For example,

The president of Carmen's firm commends her performance on a project and then offers her an account executive position. He invites her to his home for dinner to discuss the promotion. Carmen—uncomfortable about going to her boss's home after hours—tells him she is very interested in the position and suggests they meet at the office sometime during the day instead. Carmen's boss does not respond to her suggestion and later that week gives the promotion to another employee.

By making a dinner date a condition for her advancing in the firm, Carmen's boss is guilty of sexual harassment. She was offered the account executive position but when she refused the dinner invitation, Carmen's boss promoted someone else.

The second type of harassment, hostile environment, occurs when the harassing behavior of anyone in the workplace—not only a boss or supervisor—unreasonably interferes with an individual's work performance and/or causes the work environment to become hostile, intimidating, or offensive. For instance,

Susan operates a forklift in a warehouse where male co-workers post pictures from Penthouse *and* Playboy. *Her male co-workers also loudly describe pornographic films to each other in front of female co-workers. The work environment is so sexually charged that Susan—one of three women working with 45 men—feels distracted and angry a great deal of the time she is at work.*

By displaying pictures of nude women and having loud, sexually explicit conversations, Susan's male co-workers are creating a hostile and offensive work environment. They are also interfering with her ability to do her job. In other words, these men are sexually harassing Susan and other women working in the warehouse.

Sexual harassment is generally not about sexual attraction. Some offensive behavior may be misguided flirtation or inappropriate joking that was not meant to harm. And some men honestly—and mistakenly—believe patting women's backsides is appropriate workplace behavior. However, the majority of harassment is done not out of insensitivity but with the intent of making the recipient uncomfortable. The prime motivation behind most sexual harassment is to exert power over another person. Harassers are usually trying to intimidate, manipulate, or otherwise affect a person in the workplace.

While by definition both sexes can sexually harass, the most common form of harassment is men harassing women. For some men, harassment is a way to "keep women in their place." Treating women as sex objects and not as valued employees, can be an attempt to emphasize or maintain male dominance in the workplace. Men who work in predominantly male occupations may try to preserve their "boys' club" by harassing women who enter that field. Women who pursue nontraditional jobs—such as chemist, auto mechanic and sports reporter—often experience more frequent and severe sexual harassment. Rude, degrading treatment is a clear way men can communicate that women are not welcome in the workplace.

Sexual harassment is much more than a textbook description of a power play at the office. It is an experience that can seriously impact a woman's life. We can have a working knowledge of the definitions and types of sexual harassment, but until it happens to us or we explore how it *can* affect us we are only partially prepared to address the issue. Being sexually harassed can make a woman feel angry, embarrassed, humiliated, and ashamed. She may be distraught and distracted on the job and take the emotional strain home with her where it affects her family and relationships. These conditions can lead to stress-related problems such as headaches, loss of appetite, fatigue, sleeplessness, ulcers, and perhaps something as serious as clinical depression. A harassed woman may believe the situation is so bad that she must be imagining it, causing it herself, or being overly sensitive. What she may not realize is that her "extreme" reaction is a normal, "healthy" response to an outrageous situation—she is being treated with disrespect, abused, and most importantly, her economic security is being threatened.

When a woman is being sexually harassed, she often is put in the position of having to tolerate the abuse or speak out and risk her job and professional reputation. She may not report the problem at work out of fear that she will be retaliated against or not believed. Unfortunately these fears are not unfounded. Some women who come forward are dismissed as liars or emotionally unstable people. They may be transferred, demoted, or fired. In some cases, the harasser or other co-workers may retaliate by vandalizing her workspace, equipment, or car. To cope with the situation, she may use her sick leave and vacation time to avoid the harasser or ultimately choose to leave her job thereby risking a poor recommendation from her employer. A woman who is being harassed is not only paying emotionally, but may suffer high economic costs that jeopardize her financial security.

When a woman suspects she is being sexually harassed, she needs to trust her instincts. If the situation *feels* wrong, it probably *is* wrong. Doing a "reality check" with a trusted friend or co-worker can often help. She can describe the situation and ask for feedback: *What is this supposed to mean? Am I being too sensitive? Is this person abusing me?* After another person validates her concerns, she may feel more comfortable communicating her discomfort to the harasser.

The harassment is unlikely to cease without a clear message of disapproval being sent to the harasser. Fortunately, saying "no" immediately and clearly is often enough to make the harasser stop and keep the situation from escalating. The most effective response is delivered at the time of an incident and communicates what the offensive behavior is, how it makes the recipient feel, and that she wants it to stop. If talking to the harasser doesn't work or is too difficult in a given situation, a woman may choose to put her request for the behavior to stop in writing—keeping a copy for her files. For her own protection, she may also wish to document dates, times, locations, and incidents for use in an investigation or lawsuit.

If the harasser is not responsive to her requests or is somehow unapproachable (i.e., he is her supervisor or a vendor from a different company), another option is using an organization's channels for reporting harassment. Many companies and unions have designated people to discuss the issue and receive complaints. A woman can identify these individuals by consulting the organization's sexual harassment policy or asking a supervisor or someone else she trusts. Once she reaches the appropriate person, she can learn more about the company's policy and explore the process for resolving complaints. She may choose to file a formal complaint. While often a difficult step to take, informing management about sexual harassment is an increasingly effective method as more organizations acknowledge the problem. However, if in-house channels do not work or exist, there are federal, state, and local agencies with which to file complaints or there is the option of a private lawsuit.

The Equal Employment Opportunity Commission (EEOC) is the federal agency responsible for handling charges of sexual harassment in the workplace. Local EEOC offices can be found by looking in the telephone book under *US Government*. A woman working for an organization with fewer than 15 employees must file with her state or local fair-employment agency. These agencies can be found in the telephone book under state or local government.

The EEOC will ask a complainant to complete paperwork on her charges and then determine if her case meets jurisdiction requirements. If it does, the EEOC will notify the employer of the charge and perhaps hold a fact-finding conference with both parties. If an agreement between the woman and her employer cannot be reached, the EEOC will complete a full investigation to determine if there is "reasonable cause" or "no reasonable cause" to believe that harassment took place. If "reasonable cause" is found, the EEOC will work to get the employer to stop the harassment and provide remedies. In some instances, the EEOC will have its own attorneys take the case to court.

At any point in the process—even if "no reasonable cause" is found—a woman can request a "Right to Sue" letter from the EEOC that permits her to pursue a private lawsuit. Through the courts a woman can win reinstatement if she was fired, a promotion if she was denied one, back pay and attorney's fees. As a result of the Civil Rights Act of 1991, she may also collect monetary damages for her emotional suffering, medical bills, and punitive damages to punish the employer. Whether she chooses to pursue an EEOC claim or lawsuit, tries to resolve the situation in-house or otherwise, there are many support systems for a woman to use during this trying process. She may consult friends, family members, hotlines, counselors, therapists, support groups, rape-crisis centers, books—whatever might help her cope with the situation and stop the harassment.

Once we empower ourselves with knowledge about sexual harassment, we are better prepared to enter the workplace with confidence. We can pursue our goals in the world of work with an understanding of one of its hazards. If we ever encounter sexual harassment—as difficult and unpleasant as it will be—we are aware of its dangers, we are ready to respond and we will not let it derail us from our career dreams.

Colleen Phelan is the author of Sexual Harassment Solutions at Work: Profiles of Successful Policy and Practice, *published by Wider Opportunities for Women (WOW). The publication features the best practices in preventing and addressing sexual harassment of eight corporations and unions across the country. WOW is a 30-year-old nonprofit organization that works nationally as well as in its home community of Washington, DC, to achieve economic independence and equality of opportunity for women and girls.*

SUGGESTED RESOURCES

Bravo, Ellen and Ellen Cassedy. *The 9 to 5 Guide to Combating Sexual Harassment.* New York: John Wiley & Sons, Inc. 1992.

Langelan, Martha. *Back Off! How to Confront and Stop Sexual Harassment and Harassers.* New York: Simon & Schuster. 1993.

Petrocelli, William and Barbara Kate Repa. *Sexual Harassment on the Job: A Step-by-Step Guide for Working Women.* Berkeley: Nolo Press. 1992.

Phelan, Colleen. *Sexual Harassment Solutions at Work: Profiles of Successful Policy and Practice.* Washington, DC: Wider Opportunities for Women. 1992

Cinthea Fiss, 38, has been a stationary engineer for 12 years, maintaining buildings, including 52-story highrise office buildings.

STATIONARY ENGINEERS maintain machinery and operate physical plants. This includes boilers, heating, ventilation and air conditioning, pumps, electrical systems, domestic water and plumbing, emergency diesel generators, fire and life safety systems, and the automatic controls that run all of these systems. Stationary engineers work in factories, waste-water treatment plants, hospitals, hotels and office buildings. I've been working as a stationary engineer since 1982.

I learned my trade through a four-year apprenticeship program sponsored jointly by the employers and the union. The apprenticeship program is an excellent way to learn a trade because you are not expected to know anything at first. All you need is the desire to learn. Besides learning skills from journey-level engineers on the job, I also attended evening classes with the other apprentices. We studied air conditioning and refrigeration, machinery, boilers, electricity, welding, blueprint reading, safety, and the history of unions. I learned how to repair and rebuild equipment that previously I never even knew existed.

The first building I worked in was the Bank of America Headquarters in San Francisco. It is 52-stories tall, containing two-million square feet of prime financial district real estate. The engineers are responsible for the safety and comfort of about 8,000 workers. When I began, there were 18 engineers to cover shifts seven days a week, 24 hours a day.

My job always varies. One day I might be adjusting thermostats and balancing the airflow in an overheated office space, the next day I might program computerized power-demand analyzers that monitor electrical consumption and then crawl into a tiny, filthy fiberglass duct to replace a fan belt and grease a bearing. Then there are leaking pipes to repair, stopped-up drains to snake, electrical shorts, overloaded circuits, preventative maintenance on all the machinery (fans, pumps, heat exchangers, chillers, generators), toxic-chemical treatment, mechanical seals to change, pumps to rebuild, refrigeration units to repair, broken switches, and so on.

In all the high-rise office buildings I've worked in, I have always been the only female on the crew. The architecture built for male crews omits separate locker rooms. My changing facilities are often makeshift, temporary, or very distant from the shop. At one major office building, the men's locker room was in the basement next to the shop and the time clock, whereas my locker was between the 15th and 16th floors.

I believe that the sexism I confront on my job is no greater than that which women face everywhere, except that it may be more blatant in a traditionally male blue-collar job. The territory is clearly marked and gendered by photographs of

women in bikinis with power tools. Tucked between the technical manuals one can usually find *Hustler, Penthouse,* and *Soldier of Fortune.* The walls are covered with sexually explicit drawings and sexist and racist slogans. Our tools are called strippers, dykes, pliers. We work with nipples, screws, nuts, cock valves. We stick our hands inside the peckerhead, around the shaft.

Many women working in high-rise office buildings are accountants, lawyers, secretaries, and stockbrokers. By comparison to their expensive, uncomfortable clothes, I am thrilled to be able to wear a uniform, provided with laundry service by the employer, and very comfortable work boots. There is a different sense of power I feel wearing men's clothes, and knowing that I can repair and rebuild everything in the material world. I get a lot of supportive comments from women in high-rise office buildings, and many questions on how to repair this or that. Some women are interested in getting into the blue-collar trades where union contracts guarantee equality and substantial pay and benefits. I usually recommend they start with an apprenticeship program and refer them to organizations that have listings of apprenticeship programs in the area.

When I first took the test for the apprenticeship in 1980, I was looking for a skill to earn a living. It never occurred to me that being female meant something different than being male when it came to work. Although I scored high on the apprenticeship test, it took a year and a half to get hired. One of the first jobs I interviewed for was at a dairy packaging factory. The chief engineer greeted me in his office where he was drinking coffee out of a mug molded to look like a breast with a nipple spout. His first comment to me was, "I didn't think they had girls in the apprenticeship program. Well, at least I can give you a tour of the plant." After many similar interviews, I was hired at the Bank of America World Headquarters Building. Years later the chief engineer told me that he had put his job on the line by hiring me because management was greatly opposed to employing a woman. Throughout my time working there, many of my fellow engineers exclaimed that they would never hire another woman. They thought I was too much trouble.

I left that job in 1988 to work as the facilities manager at an art center. Although the pay was half my union wages, I was able to gain management skills and work in a very different environment with a female boss and co-workers. After that I've continued working in high-rise office buildings on a more temporary basis, taking time off to complete a master's program in photogra-phy. My new job as a stationary engineer is for the San Francisco Libraries. Although there are currently no women in the engineer's department, I've heard that there have been women working there before.

Last month I was in the shop, lugging huge boxes of air filters—dirty, rank filters, massive and awkward. The stench of the old filters was entrenched in my skin, woven into the polyester of my pale-blue uniform, and mingled with the salt and grime of my profuse sweat. The window cleaner, an enormous man, walked by and began to flirt with me. He called me demeaning names. As I continued my work, lugging the unwieldy filters, I briskly told him not to refer to me in such a manner. He has never spoken to me again. When I pass him, casually, and say hello, he always looks down, or away, to avoid me. But after I pass, I can feel his gaze burning holes in my back.

Martha Jane Stanton, 33, has been the team photographer for the San Francisco Giants since 1989. Stanton considers this job as "a dream come true."

WHEN PEOPLE ASK ME how I got my job as the team photographer for the San Francisco Giants, I find it hard to describe in 25 words or less. You don't go to school and major in being a team photographer. For me it was a combination of being a sports enthusiast, a photojournalist, and having a bit of business sense.

After working as a free-lance photojournalist for four years in the Bay Area, I had the opportunity to apply for the team photographer's position with the Giants. I had built a business relationship with them over the past four years and had been published in *Giants Magazine*. In 1989, I was asked to be their second photographer during the playoffs and World Series. After the season was over, their photographer retired after 18 years with the team, and I applied for the job.

Over the years I heard rumors that I got the job because I was a woman, and other rumors that I almost didn't get the job because I was a woman. I've never really known for sure, and the bottom line is, it doesn't matter. I got the job and I'm heading into my fifth season.

I've been a baseball fan for as long as I can remember. My family (my parents and seven brothers and sisters) moved from Chicago to California when I was 7 so my first memories are of

the Cubbies. But it didn't take long before I became a Giants fan. Having the job as the Giants' photographer is like a dream come true. It's the closest I can come to playing professional baseball, and it allows me to combine my love for the sport with my love for my work. My favorite part of the year is spring training. That's when I get back to the business of baseball after a four-month hiatus. Players are relaxed. Rookies emerge. Everyone is in first place.

I met manager Roger Craig at my first spring training in 1986. I remember squatting behind him, trying to get this dramatic shot when he

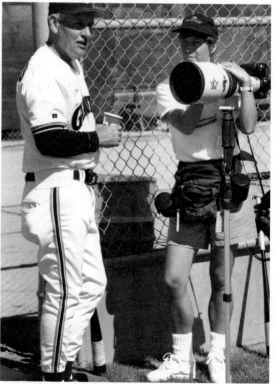

Photo: Otto Greule

offered me a chair and asked me to sit down. He asked me my name, and we've been friends ever since.

All the pictures I take for the Giants are published out of the Print/Publications Department. My photos appear in *Giants Magazine*, special book and yearbook projects, brochures, posters, and murals, etc. During the off-season, I photograph NFL football and NBA basketball for a variety of clients. Before heading to spring training every season, I vacation with my husband in Hawaii.

People talk about disadvantages in a job like mine because baseball is a man's world, but I've never felt that to be the case. Being a woman has been an advantage for me because the guys are more courteous and less likely to tell me where to go than if I were a male photographer. The only time when it is difficult on a personal level is when I have to go into the clubhouse. My job doesn't require that very often, but when I do have to go in, I do whatever it is I have to do and then I'm out of there.

I had the opportunity to be a part of a book project in the 1993 season for the Giants. I'm very proud of the book because it represents many images that I took over the course of the season. Baseball is about moments, whether it's Barry Bonds' first days as a Giant or Robby Thompson hitting a home run in the bottom of the ninth. It's my job to capture the subtle as well as the exciting. The most difficult image for me to shoot is the Giants' dejection or failure. I know for historical purposes it needs to be documented, but on the personal side, it's hard. So I have to push myself to capture those images. Though the photo may not be used by the team, I know it's there for the history books.

Photo:'Otto Greule

Jenny Harrison, 45, conducts research on motion and time. She is one of five female professors with tenure in the top ten university mathematics departments in the United States.

I STARTED OUT as a musician from the deep South, got a PhD in mathematics in England, fought a highly publicized battle over sex discrimination, and am now a professor of mathematics. So you can imagine that I have had many different and interesting experiences.

When I was a student in Alabama I always loved, and was challenged by, my mathematics classes. But it was hard for me to see what modern research mathematics was about. The depth and appeal of great music were instantly clear the first time I heard a Beethoven symphony. I dreamed of being a concert pianist and majored in music at the University of Alabama. A music professor told me that audiences preferred the male persona on stage. Since I also suffered from stage fright a change of major was in order!

I chose to study mathematics because I was intrigued by basic, unsolved questions, such as, "How can we move freely in the three spatial dimensions, but not freely in the dimension of time?" I hoped mathematics might give me the tools and language to study these questions. Much of my research has been in dynamical systems which is the study of motion and time. That first problem continues to be elusive, but I found others I could solve. I am now developing calcu-

lus for the world of fractals which includes beautiful, nonsmooth curves, surfaces, and solids. For example, think of the edge of a snowflake, the surface of your lungs, or a fern with an infinite number of small branches.

I enjoy diving deeply into research problems and thinking about them with visual aids. I like to build up a mental picture until I can see the solution. To study motion you can create an image in your mind and just watch it move around, observing what happens. There is a feeling of being driven that helps you through false leads and temporary setbacks. You are learning all the time. Then the day comes when you put the last piece into place, you see the answer, and how to get there. This feeling of discovery comes with a sense of joy that for me is proportional to the effort. Sometimes there is a gap you must fill, sometimes you find the result was known already, and sometimes no one cares. If it all comes together, you publish your discoveries and travel all over the world telling others about them.

When I entered mathematics, I believed the profession was more objective than music and would be less encumbered with bias. However, that was not to be the case. Today, in the top ten mathematics departments in this country, there are about 300 men and 5 women with tenure, including myself. Life has not been easy for any of these women. I was the first mathematician to be denied tenure at the University of California at Berkeley for more than 15 years. I sued the university for gender discrimination. The confidential records showed that I had accomplished as much as about half the men who had been promoted to tenure. Instead of going to trial, the university gave me a new review and I was awarded tenure as a full professor. This victory cost me seven years of struggle but it was well worth it. The consciousness of the academic community has been raised and many of us are working hard to make it easier for women of all ages to pursue careers in mathematics and science.

During this difficult time, I survived by networking with other women, maintaining my mathematics research, and playing chamber music with friends. I advise anyone facing difficulties to try to focus on positive activities that help you grow stronger and more confident rather than on the negative. It is better to think of constructive solutions than to play the part of the victim. A good sense of humor helps, too!

Last fall I returned to the department and was pleased to resume teaching and talking to my colleagues about research. My husband is also a professor in the department and our house is again full of "math talk." We were both changed by our political experience and are committed to helping others. By the way, I play the cello with a community orchestra and now enjoy performing. It was just a matter of time.

Photo: Raisa Fastman

Octavia E. Butler, 47, has received several awards for her science fiction (sf) writing. Among them are two Hugo Awards given by the World Science Fiction Convention and one Nebula Award given by the Science Fiction and Fantasy Writers of America.

FOR FIVE YEARS during my childhood, I lived in an apartment building that had once been a small mansion. Pasadena was full of big, old houses gone to seed in those days. I had a bedroom that had once been half a pantry. The pantry had been cut in half to give the apartment next door a bathroom. What I had left wasn't much bigger than a walk-in closet. It had a concrete floor and only one window, small and up near the ceiling. All I could see through that window were walnut tree branches and sky. In that room, seated on my bed, surrounded by my clothing and my first books, I did my earliest writing, reveling in horse stories, experimenting with romances, and finally settling in to science fiction.

I also did a lot of hiding in that room. As long as I kept out of sight, nobody expected anything of me. The older people in my family thought I was a nice, quiet kid to spend so much time in my room, out of trouble. But I knew I was hiding. I was tiresomely shy, taller than other kids my age, and thus expected to be more mature than I was. I was clumsy—probably because I was growing so fast. And I was afraid of almost everything and able to make a mess of almost anything.

At some point not long after my pantry room, the house, and the walnut tree had been cleared away to make room for a factory, I began clearing away some of my fears. I began to write consciously, deliberately about people who were afraid and who functioned in spite of their fear. People who failed sometimes and were not destroyed. No one in my earliest writings failed at anything. Their successes were as certain as my failures. But I gave my new characters my own weaknesses and tried to use those weaknesses to bring out their humanity. In my struggles to bring out their humanity, I began to come to terms with my own.

Even now, I give my characters some of my weaknesses and let them struggle toward the strengths I want to create in myself. Constructing my characters still helps me construct myself. And because I write, I'm likely to do things I might be more comfortable not doing. I deliberately allow my writer's need for experience and information to push me into new situations whether they scare me or not.

I grew up surrounded by people to whom survival itself was enough of a problem. They didn't go looking for new experiences or challenges. To them, challenge was concrete. No food, no money, no job. Because they overcame their challenges, I had the chance to be challenged by other things.

They, on the other hand, had no chance to understand why I didn't think as they did. To them, writing was, at best, a strange hobby. It

Photo: Patti Perret

kept me out of trouble. At worst, it was a waste of time and parent to my foolish delusion that I could actually earn a living by telling stories.

These people raised me. They shaped much of my world while I was growing up. I was in college before I met other kinds of people—people who learned a language, acquired a skill, created a work of art just because they wanted to. I was in college before I had even one friend who didn't either wonder why I wrote or consider my writing useless unless it made me rich. And at that time, of course, everyone knew science fiction would never make anyone rich.

As a black, a woman, the only child of a shoeshine man and a maid, I am a pretty unlikely science fiction writer. I'm probably the only black woman writing sf for a living—which caused me

a problem or two when, at 13, I began submitting stories for publication.

Most of the adult sf I had read then had as its main character a white man who was about 30 and who drank and smoked too much. So I wrote about 30-year-old white men who drank and smoked too much. But for myself, I had already begun writing the stories that later developed into my Patternist series novels—*Wild Seed, Mind of My Mind, Clay's Ark, Survivor,* and *Patternmaster.* Those were my stories. My latest story is a near-future cautionary tale called *Parable of the Sower.*

Martha Ryan, 44, is director of the Homeless Prenatal Program in San Francisco. Ryan, second from left in the photo, started the program which helps pregnant women get off drugs and welfare and turn their lives around.

MY INTEREST in other cultures began as a child growing up in Japan. That's what inspired me to study Italian and French in college and spend a year in Italy. In 1975 I had my first experience working abroad as a Peace Corps volunteer teaching English in a remote village in Ethiopia. When I left after two memorable years, I knew I wanted to return. I'd gotten back far more than I'd given.

Home again in California, I received my training as a registered nurse and worked in a busy inner-city hospital emergency room. Over the next several years, I also made three trips to Africa as a relief worker. In Somalia I started a program teaching refugee women to be community-health workers. After the training, they were able to take over many of the medical tasks on their own. In Uganda, I worked with a public-health team vaccinating children, and in Sudan, I worked with Tigrinian refugees who'd fled war-torn Ethiopia. I'll never forget the refugee camps in Sudan. At one of them, a measles epidemic killed 100 people a day. We battled outbreaks of meningitis, cholera, and hepatitis. Again, I helped train women as health-care providers in the camps.

Those experiences led me to enter a nurse practitioner program at the University of Califor-

nia at Davis and get a master's in public health from UC Berkeley, two years later. While in the program at Berkeley I volunteered with a community agency that provides health care for the homeless. The work took me to a homeless shelter where I met many pregnant homeless women who were not getting any prenatal care. I realized how few services there were for these women and how dire the consequences when they failed to get help. Often their babies were born underweight or exposed to drugs and alcohol.

I began thinking about starting a program to help these women get medical care, counseling, and other referrals needed to give their children a decent chance in life. So I took a grant-writing class and eventually got enough money to found the Homeless Prenatal Program.

Looking back, I can see how my experiences in Third World countries helped me design this program. As in Somalia and Sudan, I knew that outreach workers were the link to reach a difficult group of people needing help—populations that public agencies often give up on.

In the program's first year, we trained a number of formerly homeless women, some of whom I'd helped when I was a volunteer at the shelter. After three years, the program received additional grants and private funding. Now it is helping hundreds of homeless pregnant women have healthy babies, find housing and other services.

I'm now the full-time director of the program (I recently gave up a part-time job working in an inner-city clinic). I'm most proud of the fact that

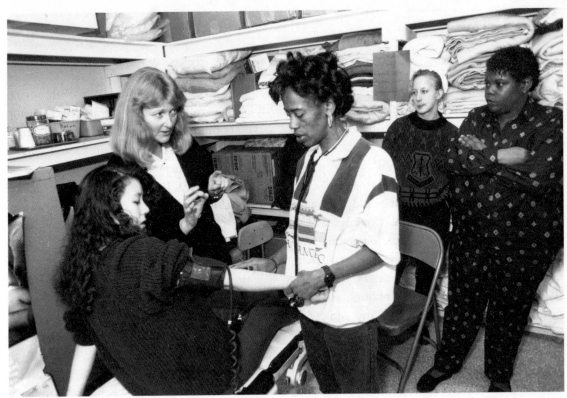

Photo: Geoffrey Hiller

we've not only helped women have healthy babies, but also helped them acquire the skills to get off welfare and move on to more productive lives. Each woman we've trained who succeeds in putting her life together becomes a role model for others. The program works and we are making a tremendous difference in this community.

COMMERCIAL PLUMBER

Teresa McClain, 42, has worked as a commercial plumber for 12 years. She has installed and secured new plumbing in a wide array of structures, including high-rise office buildings, hospitals, airports, sewage treatment plants, and hotels.

I'M A RECOVERING addict and alcoholic so my life is about yearning for more. My inability to accept the norm, the commonplace, drove me to find something to do for a living that is different and constantly changing. I didn't want to wear a dress, type, answer phones, etc., ad infinitum. It seems that part of my addictive makeup is that I grow restless in any situation after about a year. So, I went to a library and read about various trades. I was drawn to commercial plumbing and operating engineering. In both trades I'd be using my mind and body, I wouldn't face the same job or people every day, and each project was not long term. I applied for both apprenticeships and was called to the plumbers' union first.

When I went on my first job site it was like a dream come true. My addictive personality and low self-esteem, honed from childhood, found a haven. Here were men; all shapes, sizes, colors, and all interested in me! Without a strong sense of self, I adapted perfectly to whatever they wanted me to be. I could be the sweet daughter, the pal (either sisterly or vulgar) or the sex object. The essential element was that they like me. I whisked through a few years this way but then got caught in the impossible dilemma of staying the "sweet daughter" to some, while having sex with others. My alcoholism soared at this time. My behavior and inner turmoil were annihilating me. I sobered up, got a divorce, bought a house, and started changing. I was then able to look at my career as just that. The way I intended to make my living for some time to come. I realized my focus was not on my plumbing skills although I worked hard to make up for being small and I did great in school.

During the second year of my apprenticeship I noticed that my classmates (all male) seemed to know a lot more than I did on the job sites. When asked if we knew how to do some task, most of the guys said yes and I said no. I knew I was sharp, had good ideas that I voiced, and did good work, but I still felt left behind. My feelings of inadequacy started taking over. After some time I started to ask my classmates questions. I found that most of them said yes, they knew how to do something, and then faked it. I always said no until I had asked enough questions to be sure I could do the task at hand. I realized that all our journeymen were taught the "fake it" method. Consequently, I usually stood out like a sore thumb. I wanted explanations. This made it really hard for me.

I sobered up three-and-a-half years into my apprenticeship. This was essential for trying to gain confidence in myself. I had quite a difficult time trying to switch my self-esteem from being fed from the outside to growing from the inside. I had to accept that I seem to think differently from most of my co-workers, but that's OK. I ask lots of questions till I have the task straight in my mind rather than just forging ahead, which is typical of my peers. I have learned to accept that my way is just fine. I'm smart and capable but different. My ideas, work skills, and capabilities were always up to par but my self-confidence and self-esteem always needed a lot of nurturing.

I make almost $26 an hour, but I work hard. My job entails getting the blueprints for a building, and laying the piping accordingly. When I run the pipe up or down the walls, I then have to hook up the fixtures—drinking fountains, floor drains, toilets, ice makers, hot water tanks, etc. In the end, I must test the piping system to be sure there are no leaks. I use all kinds of power tools, run lots of equipment like forklifts and truck cranes. And I solder and braze copper and brass pipe fittings, and I weld supports. This is a very simplified version of my job.

My nine years of sobriety and nearly 13 years in the plumbing trade have given me quite a sense of accomplishment. I never thought I'd stick to anything for this long. The changes in job sites, companies, and co-workers have helped a lot in my ability to stick it out. I never stay in one place long enough to get thoroughly tired of it. Another plus is that I feel I can take care of myself both financially and in everyday tasks. If something breaks I can take it apart and fix it, or I can afford to have someone else do it. I have a lot more choices in my life today. I make enough money to do nearly anything I want. This has been a great ego booster and liberator.

Photo: Nancy Clendaniel

Kathryn Brigham, 47, fishes for a living, along with her three daughters. Brigham is also the alternate commissioner for the United States section of the Pacific Salmon Commission, representing the 24 tribes in Oregon, Washington, and Idaho affected by the Pacific Salmon Treaty.

I AM a member of the Confederated Tribes of the Umatilla Reservation located east of Pendleton, Oregon. I have two brothers and two sisters who live on the reservation and one brother who is a fisherman on the Columbia River. We were raised on the reservation. We learned that we all need to co-exist with our natural resources, although at the time I didn't really know that was what my parents and grandparents were teaching me. Many times it was a game we played. For example, when we went camping to pick berries our camp ground had to be cleaned before we set up camp. Before leaving our campsite Dad had us see if we could leave our campsite looking as if no one had been there. Dad brushed away our tracks, leaving the site cleaner than when we got there. We were told it was important to keep our land, water, and air clean because we depend on our natural resources. We were also taught to gather our food in a manner that would not wipe it out and only gather what we need.

I never thought I would become involved in tribal government and work with state and federal agencies to protect our natural resources for our

children and their children's children. I believed that when I grew up I was going to be a housewife, stay home, and take care of my family.

My husband, a Umatilla tribal fisherman, has fished on the Columbia River since he was 8 years old. We have three daughters and two granddaughters. My daughters and I fish. We have our own boat and fishing gear, which we hang, run, clean, and patch ourselves. During the summer months we can fish with our hoop nets and we only use our gillnets during the tribal fall commercial season. Our tribal gillnets can be up to 400 feet in length and must be run each day to take the fish out of the net. It is important to take care of our fish or get them to the buyers as soon as possible.

In the summer of 1976 the Umatilla Fish and Wildlife Committee had a vacancy. My first years on the committee were very easy because my grandpa was a well-respected tribal leader of 48 years who relied on me to do a lot of work for him. We would sit down together and discuss the different options available to the tribe. I had to explain the pros and cons of each option and grandpa asked for my recommendation and why. Once we reached an agreement on an approach, Grandpa then presented it to the Fish and Wildlife Committee or the Board of Trustees for tribal support. Very seldom did the tribe do something different. I was very lucky to work with my grandpa for two years before he passed away.

Once he was gone I had to learn to do these things myself through the Umatilla Tribe. Outside

Photo: Angela Pancrazio

the tribe it was very difficult because my recommendations were often turned down because I am a woman. Some tribes believe that women should be at home rather than be involved in planning or decision-making processes. This tribal view may never change. Therefore, I have chosen to do the best I can to fight to make things better for our children and their children's children.

When I represented the Umatilla Fish and Wildlife Committee and the Columbia River Inter-Tribal Fish Commission I learned that the state and federal agencies have real problems making changes even though the changes are better for our natural resources. Most programs are based on today's needs and what the public can get from our natural resources now. Some agencies are more concerned about protecting today's jobs and the power to say "no" versus trying to develop a coordinated approach to rebuilding, protecting, and enhancing our natural resources. They are not looking at what the future is holding. Unless there is better accountability by all agencies to co-exist with our natural resources, the resources will continue to decline. Our children will have only pictures.

I am not afraid of hard work or asking for help. I enjoy working with people and I believe it is important to keep your word, be truthful, and respect people. Therefore, I am very disappointed when people are not truthful with me and do things that are underhanded.

The reward I want from my work is for things to be better for my grandchildren and their children's children. I feel good when someone tells me I have done a good job, or when I believe I have done a good job.

Right now I am the first and only woman alternate commissioner in the United States section of the Pacific Salmon Commission working with Canada. The US Tribal Alternate Commissioner and Tribal Commissioner represent the 24 tribes in Oregon, Washington, and Idaho affected by the Pacific Salmon Treaty. It is very difficult at times, but I want to see the tribes, state and federal agencies accept responsibility, and to be accountable by developing a coordinated approach so our children and their children's children will have our natural resources in the future.

Terry Cruz-Johnson, 50, says farming is very hard work, but she can't imagine doing anything else because of the freedom and independence she has with her work.

I LIVE AND WORK on a vegetable farm that has been in my family for 50 years. As a young girl thinking about what I wanted to be when I grew up, I knew that I did not want to work on a farm. I thought a nine-to-five job would be a better profession. Now, I can't imagine doing anything else but farming. The farm has always been a family affair. I helped my dad in the fields as I was growing up. Now he is 83 years old and he helps *me* in the fields, and my mother sells the vegetables we grow at the marketplace. I like being on the farm because of the freedom and independence it gives my husband and me. It was a wonderful place to raise my son and daughter, and it is a great environment for my grandson as he grows.

Farming is very hard work. From spring through fall my days are long and filled with lots of work. A typical day is up early, and right after breakfast and morning chores I start the crew. I make the decisions of what to pick and how much is needed for the stand, and to deliver the goods to the marketplace each day. Once I have the crew picking, it is time to open the stand and start the customers in the U-pick field. The stand and field are open until 6 p.m., then I unload the empty boxes from the truck returning from market. After that, I return to the house and work on the never-ending book work and chores. By the end of the evening, I am ready to go to bed.

I really enjoy working with customers. It is a challenge for me to learn their names or something about them so I will remember them. The people who U-pick are very friendly and enjoyable to be around. One of the challenges is trying to explain to customers when something didn't grow right because it was too hot or too wet.

The farm is a wonderful place to live and work. The open space, fresh air, and the feel of the soil are things that I will never give up. It is very tiring and demanding work in the summer, but it is what I have always done and I truly enjoy it.

Photo: Gary Kissel

Valerie Simmons Arnold, 34, has been a police officer since 1979. She was rated the best in her police academy class in firearms, second place academically, and the top woman in physical training. Arnold says police work is "in her blood." However, the death of her brother, also a law enforcement officer, profoundly affected her, becoming what she describes as a transforming event.

THE FIRST THING most people ask me when they learn that I am a police officer is, "What made you want to be a police officer?" There are several reasons. First, it was a challenge for me; women weren't supposed to do a "man's job," so I wanted to see if I could do it—I could! Second, I felt that I could help others—not change the world, but help. Third, I liked the possibilities for variety. I have learned there's not much time for boredom, unless you work the 11 p.m. to 7 a.m. shift on a Sunday.

During my career I've developed a lot of confidence in myself. I've seen things that I hope I never have to see again. I've seen a lot of sad out there like a mother shot down by her husband while she was holding her 4-year-old son's hand. How do you explain that to a child? I saw a 3-year-old boy run over by a dump truck. He didn't even look injured, but died later of internal injuries. I've seen several fatalities (car accidents) and thank God, I didn't have to deliver the death messages. There's a lot of pain in this, but I still feel a need to be out there. Sometimes dealing with it is hard, but I've got good friends and close

family to talk to about it. The hardest for me is seeing elderly people and children hurt. I think all police officers are that way. I've cried about some of my cases, sometimes when I'm off duty. You've got to be able to release it.

Since I was hired in February of 1979, I have worked in Criminal Records, Sex Crimes Detective Division, Building Security, Undercover Metro Division, and Uniform Patrol. At one point, I went to Metro Division on a temporary assignment, undercover, buying drugs. I guess I was the guinea pig. I'd buy and the guys would come in behind me and make the bust.

In recent years my life has been reshaped by profound grief in the tragic death of my brother, and immeasurable love at the birth of each of my children. My transformation began on January 14, 1988 with the birth of my first son, Cade Brandon. At that time I was single and although the pregnancy was unplanned, Cade was the light of my life. I drew strength during that time from the support of my family. My brother, Jerry, moved into my house to help me. He was also a law enforcement officer in East Baton Rouge, Narcotics Division. On November 21, 1988, Jerry was shot and killed in a drug bust when he burst through the door of a hotel room where two undercover personnel were being threatened by a drug dealer. Jerry was given a hero's funeral and posthumously received several medals, including the Medal of Valor for saving the lives of the other two agents.

Returning to police work after my brother's

death was extremely difficult. At the time, my department had no program to help me deal with my grief. However, I found out about Concerns of Police Survivors (COPS), a national support group, and for the first time found someone who understood how I felt. They were the lifeline I needed to cope, and I am still very active with the group. In the year following Jerry's death I met my husband. He was so sensitive and caring that I knew he was the one I wanted to spend my life with. We now have another son, and finally, a baby girl.

I have been on the police department for 15 years. Currently I am assigned to the Impound Division where we deal with abandoned vehicles, auto thefts and recoveries, vehicle evidence, and wrecker regulations. Police work is still in my blood and I am very pleased with my career, but my husband and children have top priority in my life now. My younger sister joined the police department two years ago. Yes, I worry about her, but she had good training and I have to trust that God will watch over her. I also have two older sisters, and they are school teachers.

My parents and our family have always been close, but after losing Jerry we realize even more how important it is to treasure the times that we have together. I have learned that life is a precious gift and all too often we take for granted what we have been given. If we have an opportunity to help someone or to tell someone that we love them, we should never let that chance pass us by. It may never come again.

Photo: Mark Saltz

CHIEF MATE

Karin M. Johnson, 45, works for the Washington State Ferry System piloting a ferry boat in Puget Sound. As second in command, she is also responsible for the training and safety of all crew members as well as maintenance of the vessel.

AS A NATIVE of Washington State, I've always been kind of a thrill seeker, drawn to all sorts of out-door activities, including sky diving, skiing, scuba diving, and even mountain climbing. (I celebrated my 30th birthday by climbing Mt. Rainier with a professional mountain climber leading the way!) But it was my job down at the Pike Street Market in Seattle, working for the Preservation and Development Authority, that led to my current, 15-year stint with the Washington State Ferry System. In 1979, the Hood Canal Bridge blew down so there was this sudden need for additional people to staff the ferries. I inquired about a position and the timing couldn't have been better. After five years of watching the ferries go back and forth across Puget Sound while working a desk job at Pike Place Market, I was hired on as an ordinary seaman and was finally on the water myself.

My irregular work schedule resulted in a somewhat irregular child-rearing arrangement between me and my ex-husband in the day-to-day responsibilities of raising our daughter, Anya, who is now 21 years old. I focused on working my way up through the system: from ordinary seaman, to able seaman, and on to my present position as chief mate with a captain's license. My income now allows me to support myself and my daughter comfortably.

Although there are many wonderful aspects about piloting a ferry boat, including being privy to the particularly magnificent Pacific Northwest sunrises and sunsets, ferry boating isn't for everyone. There are constant challenges presented by the tide, the wind, and the current. Work schedules are still irregular, often making it necessary for me to spend off-hours on board. Shifts can range from 4 a.m. to noon, or from noon to 8 p.m., and variations thereof. Working weekends and most holidays can definitely eliminate any type of social life outside of work. But the satisfaction I gain from becoming competent in navigation and ship handling makes it all worthwhile.

Every woman who has worked in a nontraditional, male-dominated workplace has, I believe, encountered some type of sexual harassment. Ferry boating is no exception. I think that nowadays women have supported each other by taking a firm stand against being victims of violence in the work environment. Now it is time for men who observe this sexist behavior to voice their disapproval. By remaining silent, they actually continue to promote the violation and degradation of all women. With this in mind, I have always encouraged my crew members to speak out against any injustice they encounter on the job.

As a chief mate, I am second in command. I follow the captain's orders while the crew follows

my orders. I am directly responsible for the training and safety of all crew members, as well as overseeing the maintenance of the vessel, loading the vessel, and standing watch on the bridge on an alternating basis. I am also responsible for handling all pay orders and ordering supplies. While the first mate handles a lot of the same duties as the captain, plus the crew, the ultimate responsibility lies with the captain, whose seniority reflects his or her title and skill at the helm.

As I believe in the necessity for growth and learning even at the top of any field, it has been my dream while working aboard the Washington State ferries to become even more effective and proficient as a ship handler. I hope that some day all this hard work, backed up by an inquisitive mind, and a good sense of humor, will earn me the title of "captain."

Joyce Shon, 37, has been a heavy-equipment operator for public works for the past 12 years.

TO GO ALL the way back, I got into this line of work by the accident of being the second child and the second daughter. Big sister was already apprenticed with Mom in the (then) acceptable art of household management. Therefore, when I (my first big failure!) proved not to be the expected son, I became Dad's #1 assistant. And there was lots to do in a new house on a tight budget. To be fair, everybody helped with everything. We built retaining walls, landscaped, put in watering systems, poured concrete patios and paths, and kept the old Plymouth station wagon running. In those cold-war days, we even built a fallout shelter! With such a variety of activities as a child, it's not surprising that I never felt restricted by "traditional."

The public works field was not an easy career to get into for a woman, but public awareness of women's rights in the 1970s definitely helped, and assistance from government agencies was available. I doubt I could have done it otherwise. Always, and still, there are difficulties on the daily work level, such as resistance from many men to the invasion of their territory. Being a small minority of the work force makes you very obvious and subject to close scrutiny/criticism from skeptical co-workers. Men are people too, I remind myself. Some have been wonderful, patient, helpful, informative, supportive. And some have been dreadful, the archetypal macho-sexist type! With the latter, I eventually discovered that their hostility isn't necessarily personal, it seems consistently to stem from their own insecurities! I've refused to let their problems become mine—I like to feel good about myself! I've learned that a solid belief in my own competence is a necessary foundation to other people acknowledging it.

As an equipment operator, I am a very obvious part of a crew, both to co-workers and the public. One of the hardest things for me has been overcoming a fear of trying new techniques or equipment in front of an audience. No miracle cures or short cuts to offer here—just keep at it! I've seen so many women leave this field, overwhelmed by dealing with nonfamiliar work and outdated attitudes towards women. And worse, sorry to report, some women expect special privileges because they are women...well, women are people too! They make it harder for competent women to earn respect and recognition.

Some guidelines I developed for myself to survive: (1) Be conscientious about your work; (2) Be patient and persistent with yourself when learning new skills; (3) Be realistic about working in male territory—you're going to be hustled, harassed, unfairly criticized, and even sabotaged by an unpleasant group. You're probably not going to change their attitudes and beliefs no matter how good you are; (4) Keep your self-respect in good working order; (5) Most importantly, keep your sense of humor. There are going to be times when nothing else will keep you going—great advice from my mother. And then there are those pay-off times, a difficult job well done by group effort gives a sense of achievement and camaraderie.

I've found minor aggravations can get to me more than major issues. I canceled a subscription to a magazine that professed to address all the concerns of working mothers over a beauty column. First, there were endless covers of perfectly coifed, dress-for-success moms with beribboned and ruffled daughters, never a pair of coveralls or hard hat. And then the ultimate insult—how to overcome the devastating effects of conditioned office air on complexion and hair. I nearly sent them a treatise on how to clean a face blackened with dust and diesel fumes; salvage a hairdo ravaged by long sweaty hours mashed under a hard hat; how to make stained and callused hands presentable on a date; and just exactly what do you wear that won't call attention to the sunburned lines on your neck and arms.

I've been told that it's a "personal problem." Steel-toe boots, gloves, rainwear, coveralls, and such required safety equipment are not provided in sizes to fit a 5'1" person with hips and breasts! But despite the problems, big and small, I like my job. I especially like the self-respect I've earned while overcoming obstacles and mastering skills.

Photo: Ann Meredith

NONTRADITIONAL JOBS FOR WOMEN

KRISTIN WATKINS

WHEN WOMEN think about nontraditional jobs, they usually think of construction work—carpenters, electricians, and plumbers. What women don't consider are a full range of jobs such as copy-machine repairer, water-treatment plant operator, or drafter. In fact, most jobs are nontraditional for women, since women are concentrated in only 20 out of 440 broad occupational classifications. Nontraditional jobs are considered any occupation where women are less than 25 percent of the workers.

There is a perception in American society that women have made great strides in the workplace and that they are now represented in significant numbers in all types of jobs. In fact, only a small percentage of women work in nontraditional occupations. These nontraditional jobs are primarily in professional occupations such as doctor and lawyer. Statistics for 1992 show that women were 20.4 percent of employed doctors and 21.4 percent of employed lawyers. In contrast, only 1.2 percent of electricians, 10.5 percent of telephone installers, 4.6 percent of truck drivers, and .8 percent of auto mechanics were women.

In 1992, women working as mechanics earned $523 a week, while women working as data entry clerks earned only $344. What's different about these jobs? One difference is who works in them. Women make up 85 percent of all data entry clerks, making this traditional women's work, and only 3 percent of mechanics, which is considered nontraditional.

Why is it important for women to have a chance in male-dominated occupations? The primary reason is economic self-sufficiency. Women are too often unable to support themselves and their families by working in low-paying, traditionally female jobs such as child-care worker, nursing assistant, and cashier. A salary of $523 a week goes a lot farther than $344. Nontraditional jobs typically pay 30 percent more than traditional female jobs. Most nontraditional occupations also have established career ladders and provide on-the-job training. Traditionally, female occupations often require additional education for career advancement. For example, a copy-machine repair technician can earn $17 an hour as a trainee and can advance to $22 as a field technician, but a nursing assistant interested in increasing her salary must go to college to obtain her nursing degree.

Just like men, women's interests and abilities are diverse. Some women take great pride and enjoyment in building or repairing things. Women working in nontraditional jobs often have worked in traditionally female jobs but were unhappy with the work. Working in nontraditional jobs increases their self-esteem and job satisfaction. Women in the construction trades can drive by a building with their kids and say, "Mom helped build that!" Many women also prefer working outdoors in jobs such as surveyor or phone installer, where everyone's "office" has a window. Nontraditional jobs often offer greater independence: a locksmith or a truck driver maps out her own work day and schedule. Many non-traditional jobs are characterized by less supervision and more autonomy than traditional female jobs.

Seventy-three percent of women work in non-professional occupations. However, the number of women working in the blue-collar trades and technical occupations has remained small over the past few years. Thus, the wage gap between men and women continues to be large. As of 1994 that wage gap is about 75 cents to the dollar. Women continue to lag in blue-collar and technical jobs for a variety of reasons:

—Women's lack of familiarity with the blue-collar jobs. While many young men may have helped their fathers work on the car, most young women helped their mothers clean the house. Subsequently, many women cannot picture what an auto mechanic does and are unfamiliar with mechanical work. Few women are likely to know what a computerized machine tooler does (they operate machines programmed by computers to cut metal parts for airplanes, appliances and other products), or what an electrical-line mechanic does (they fix and maintain electric-utility cables). In contrast, if you ask women what a nurse or a secretary does, most will be able to tell you.

— Most women and girls do not know other women who have worked in these jobs and cannot imagine themselves in these roles. Role models for women and girls considering their job options are essential.

—Guidance and employment counselors may not suggest a career in welding or firefighting to their female students or clients, thinking it more appropriate for women and girls to pursue clerical courses rather than trade and protective service careers.

—Some women have found it difficult to work in nontraditional jobs because they have faced sexual harassment. A study conducted in the 1980s by Wider Opportunities for Women (WOW), a national women's organization focusing on employment and training issues, found that 98 percent of tradeswomen surveyed had experienced sexual harassment.

—The lack of basic pre-vocational skills needed for a nontraditional career may deter some women from pursuing nontraditional work. They may fear math, a requirement for most technical and trade occupations. Or they may be unfamiliar with tools, or may not be used to doing the heavy lifting that some nontraditional jobs require.

—Others may not find the support they need from family and friends. Parents, in particular, may not think that nontraditional jobs are appropriate for their daughters.

STRATEGIES FOR NONTRADITIONAL WORK

There are effective strategies to help women enter nontraditional jobs by preparing both the women themselves and the workplace.

Women interested in finding out more about nontraditional occupations can peruse *Occupational Outlook Quarterly*, available at local libraries.

This US Department of Labor publication describes the training needed and what the work is like for many different jobs. They can also contact the human resources department of an employer in a nontraditional field or a union apprenticeship director and ask them for referrals of women already working in nontraditional jobs in their companies or unions. A woman can also ask the employer about the possibility of doing a job shadow, where she is paired with an employee for a few hours to observe what the work is like. Perhaps she can try out the job—maybe lay some cable or climb scaffolding. Union apprenticeship directors may also be willing to facilitate job shadowing opportunities. finally, women can do some research to see if there is a support group for women in nontraditional jobs in their communities where they can learn about job opportunities and strategies for pursuing nontraditional work. A good place to start is to call the US Department of Labor, Women's Bureau for their region.

Education and job training systems can focus on recruiting women for nontraditional jobs by providing them with career information and access to female role models. They also can link women with support groups for women in the trades and technical occupations. Job-training programs can teach women how to handle sexual harassment, and help them develop their physical strength, math aptitude, and tool identification skills. Employers and unions can be prepared to integrate women into nontraditional worksites by preventing isolation and providing appropriate changing facilities and bathrooms. Employers also can take an active role in preventing sexual harassment, including sending a strong message to

AVERAGE WEEKLY WAGES FOR NONTRADITIONAL JOBS

Telephone Installer and Repairer	$656
Tool & Die Maker	$642
Firefighter	$636
Data Processing Equipment Repairer	$619
Stationary Engineer	$618
Police Officer & Detective	$615
Aircraft Engine Mechanic	$606
Millwright	$594
Electrical & Electronic Technician	$593
Crane & Tower Operator	$570
Drafter	$527
Plumber, Pipefitter, & Steamfitter	$518
Heavy Equipment Mechanic	$516
Operating Engineer	$514
Sewage Treatment Plant Operator	$503

These are the average weekly wages for both women and men prepared by the Bureau of Labor Statistics (BLS) from 1992 data. The BLS is unable to obtain data on women's wages in many nontraditional jobs simply because there are so few women who work in them.

employees and management that sexual harassment will not be tolerated.

Successful efforts to train and place women in nontraditional jobs are occurring throughout the United States. For example, in 1991 the Nontraditional Employment for Women Act (NEW) was passed, requiring for the first time that states and local job training councils set goals for training women and girls in nontraditional jobs, and to evaluate their progress in meeting those goals.

Anticipating the passage of this legislation, Wider Opportunities for Women launched the Nontraditional Employment Training (NET) project to help increase women's access to nontraditional training and well-paid jobs through the mainstream job training system. The NET Project assists a local leadership team composed of job training and vocational education administrators, employers, unions, apprenticeship officials, state legislators, tradeswomen, and others. All these groups work together to make the changes in the job-training system necessary to train women for nontraditional jobs.

After two years, the accomplishments of the project have been significant. In the project's Montana demonstration site, 60 women have been trained for nontraditional jobs at an average hourly wage of $9.51. The jobs included heavy-equipment operator, soil tester, and truck driver. In Milwaukee, over 88 women have chosen a nontraditional occupation as a career goal, and many have already been placed in nontraditional jobs such as computerized-machine tooler, welder, and construction-crew supervisor, with these jobs paying an average wage of $8.69 an hour.

These efforts show that women are interested in working at male-dominated jobs and are willing to deal with the negatives such as sexual harassment in order to earn higher wages and enjoy expanded career opportunities. If women continue to be concentrated in low-paying, traditionally female jobs, they will never truly be able to support themselves and their families. For many, a nontraditional job can mean the difference between poverty and economic self-sufficiency.

Kristin Watkins is the program associate for the Nontraditional Employment Training (NET) Project of Wider Opportunities for Women (WOW) in Washington, DC. She also provides key support for WOW's public policy work in nontraditional employment for women.

RESOURCES

The following materials on nontraditional occupations for women are available at Wider Opportunities for Women, 1325 G Street NW, Washington, DC, 20005. (202-638-3143).

Nontraditional Occupations for Women. A bibliography published by WOW lists the best materials available on the subject, including videos, newsletters, and reports.

Women and Nontraditional Work Factsheet. Published by WOW; gives a statistical profile of women employed in nontraditional occupations, outlines public policy relating to nontraditional occupations, and provides an overview of the barriers and strategies to improve women's employment in these fields.

Consider a Nontraditional Job is an upbeat video produced by WOW targeted toward women living in rural areas. Viewers learn what the work is like, what type of work environment can be expected, and the benefits and barriers of pursuing a nontraditional job.

Mythbusters. A video for young women considering high-paying nontraditional careers. Hosted by three female teenagers of color, the video leads viewers through a series of myths about nontraditional work for women and explains why the myths are not valid. This video is available through Middlesex County Vo-Tech, 618 New Brunswick Avenue, Perth Amboy, NJ 08861. (908-442-9595).

Juanita H. Ellithorpe, 41, has been in the military almost 20 years. Ellithorpe is the only woman out of 21 command sergeant majors at Ft. Lewis, Washington and oversees more than 300 military personnel.

WHEN I WAS 22-years old, I was lured by the famous recruitment slogan: "Join Up and See the World!" So I enlisted. My first year in the military became a year of major change in what I thought of myself and what I expected from life. My recruiter sold me on the idea of being a munitions specialist; inspecting, renovating, and building all types of munitions. He said it would be a life of excitement, travel, and glamour (yes, I know). Well, my vision of traveling and seeing the world amounted to assignments in the States that included Georgia, Kentucky, Alabama, North Carolina, Texas, Hawaii, Colorado, and Washington. Hardly the dreams of traveling that I had imagined!

My first assignment was in Georgia on an installation referred to as a retirement post. In my unit, I was the first and only female soldier for nearly a year (talk about breaking new trails!). My commander made it clear I was not welcome and I shouldn't even unpack my bags. No one was allowed to talk to me, but that did not stop them from talking around me. I do believe I heard just about everyone's version of his sexual "prowess" and what I was missing. (In those days, it was believed that women only went into the service for one of three reasons: looking for a husband, sexually active, or because of sexual preference). I spent more time in the ammunition supply point pondering my situation (and counting bullets) than I did around other soldiers. This is not to say all soldiers were in this category because there were those who tried to protect me.

Despite my misery that first year, and better judgment, I decided to stay in. When I look back, I have to admit I acquired a strength, understanding, and acceptance that helped me to cope throughout my military career. I learned to laugh when things were unbearable. There was no way I was going to cry in front of anyone or give my adversary the satisfaction of knowing he/she was getting to me. This was the inner strength (as the military says, intestinal fortitude) that got me through the tough times. One story that stands out occurred when I was being qualified for air assault. I was the only female in the unit (again!) and drew a lot of attention. I worked as a parachute rigger and every instructor made a point of hollering my student ID number. When I answered, I heard the famous words: "Drop!" This means ten push-ups on the spot. I was such a favorite for this command that I even had my own designated "PU" (push-up) spot. The other guys in the course said they were going to have my handprints bronzed at the location where I spent most of my time in the "front-leaning rest" position. So, you can either take all of this in and cop a negative attitude or you can apply it toward building character, which is the road I chose.

I've seen a lot over the years—from one ex-

Photo: Nancy Clendaniel

treme to the other. At one point women were discriminated against because that was the way men and women were raised. Now we're on the losing end because of a few women who abuse the programs implemented to protect women, and who hide their incompetence and lack of standards behind a smoke screen. They fail to understand that all women are judged by the actions of a few, and unfortunately we're compared to those who create a negative impression.

The one element you have that no one can take away, the one element you must use to judge people with, and to be judged by, is integrity. A person who is willing to compromise her/his integrity has no moral standards. A person who has no moral standards is an individual who will say or do whatever is necessary to get ahead, no matter who is hurt in the process. Once you have compromised your integrity, there is no getting it back! This is a guaranteed path to failure.

With just about 20 years in the military, I have done quite well for myself. I've never compromised my integrity, and always kept an open mind about people and situations, knowing that people can be vicious with rumors.

I am an E-9 now, command sergeant major (CSM), not to be confused with sergeant major (SGM). There is only one other position higher that would be nice to attain, and that is command sergeant major of the Army. There is only one position with that title. Time has not changed that much yet. For a while, only men will be selected for that position. And, for a while, that may be the best choice for the Army. Then again, Command Sergeant Major of the Army Ellithorpe has a nice ring to it—don't you think?

HOSPITAL AIDE

Mary Ann Wiggins, 32, worked as a hospital aide for ten years at a developmental center for the mentally retarded. After a divorce, she took time off to spend with her children. She is now a private duty nurse's aide.

I STARTED WORKING as a hospital aide about ten years ago. I really enjoyed working at a developmental center because it was a challenge. It gave me a chance to help where I was needed. It was fun, there were good times, and also bad times. There were some people you could help, and there were some you couldn't help other than to make them as comfortable as possible. This is a very emotional job because you deal with all types of residents as well as families. When I first started working as a hospital aide, my duties included caring for patients—toileting, feeding, grooming, and oral hygiene. Later on, I was a therapeutic program worker, which meant I did the shopping for all the residents' needs or requests. I also dealt with concerned parents, which I enjoyed. I traveled 30 miles each way, everyday, to get to my work.

The most important reason I left the developmental center after ten years was for the rest. But also, I went through a divorce, leaving me with two children who are almost teenagers. We had a whole new adjustment to contend with. Being a hospital aide sometimes caused emotionally depressing days. Plus, I was going through depressing times at home. Besides, my children and I needed to get to know each other again. It's hard

being a mother and a father to teenage children, mentally and financially, but I enjoy it. Through all my ups and downs, I have my mother at my side, encouraging and praying for me, just being there for support. She also works at the same developmental center. Now, I've got my life together. My children are ready to take on life. I'm working again as a private duty nurse's aide for the elderly and I enjoy it. I have a new love in my life. I can honestly say I am a strong-willed working woman. Someday, I hope to be a certified nurse.

Meridel LeSueur, 94, has been a writer most of her life. She wrote this piece for the first edition of Women & Work *in 1986. LeSueur now lives with her daughter in Wisconsin.*

WHEN I WAS 10 years old in 1910 I knew my two brothers could be anything they wanted. I knew I could be a wife and mother, a teacher, a nurse or a whore. And without an education, I could not be a nurse or teacher and we were very poor. Women could be china painters, quiltmakers, embroiderers. They often wrote secretly. Even read certain books secretly. My mother tried to go to college and women could not take math or history, only the domestic sciences.

I began to write down what I heard, sitting under the quilting frames. I tried to listen to these imprisoned and silenced women. I had a passion to be witness and recorder of the hidden, submerged, and silent women. I did not want to be a writer; I did not know a woman writer; I did not read a woman writer. It was a thick, heavy silence and I began to take down what I heard.

My Gramma hated my writing. "We have tried to hide what has happened to us," she said, "and now you are going to tell it." "I am. I am going to tell it," I cried, and I began a long howl and cry that finally found its voice in the women's movement, as it is called. A book I wrote in 1930, cruelly criticized by male editors, was not published until 1975. My audience was women, who now wanted to talk, bear witness.

I made my living working in factories, writing for the labor movement. A good thing for a writer to keep close to life, to the happening, and I have lived in the most brutal century of two world wars, millions killed and exploited, and now the atom bomb and the global struggle.

I went to the International Women's Conference in Nairobi at 85 years old to see the thousands of women now bearing their own witness and I read my poem *Solidarity*, which I wrote for the Vietnamese Women's Union, and it was translated at once into Swahili as I read it. A great climax to my life. I believe this is the most enlightened moment I have seen in history and rooted in my life's passion to bear witness to the common struggle, the heroic people rising out of the violence, all becoming visible and alive.

My struggle was never alone, always with others. This makes my life bright with comradeship, marches with banners, tribal courage, and warmth. Remember, I didn't vote 'til I was 19 in 1919. Women only came into the offices after the first World War. Every young man I knew in high school never returned. The fathers and husbands had been killed. A terrible reaction set in after that bloody war to consolidate patriarchal money and power. The twenties were a terrible sinking into the Depression.

My mother, wanting to be an actress, sent me to dramatic school. I tried to fulfill her desires. The theater then was developing actresses who exploited the sexist feminine, and males who had

Photo: Margaret Randall

to be John Waynes. The plays were also made for this image of sexism. Coming from the prairies, I played *Lady Windermere's Fan* by Oscar Wilde, learning to walk and use a fan and speak Britain. I didn't cotton to that at all. I went to Hollywood where again, your career was based on sexism, the female stereotypes. You had to go every morning to the hiring hall and show your legs and teeth and get a job for the day signing a contract that if you were killed or injured the company would not be responsible. Many extras were killed. You

were a dime a dozen and the studios were flooded with the beautiful prairie girls from the Midwest. It was a meat market and developed one of the greatest prostitute rings in Los Angeles, San Francisco, Seattle, and Las Vegas.

My first job was to jump off a burning ship into salt water with dangerous tides. I lived. You could make $25 a day, an enormous sum, and I could save it and hole in and write for a few months. So I began to write about the open market on women; cheap labor of women, oppression and silencing and bartering of women. Also, fighting in the unions and housing. In the Depression, women were not on any list. There were no soup kitchens for women. Also, there was the danger of sterilization. Groups of women were netted and taken to women's prisons and might be sterilized by morning. There was a theory that the only solution to the Depression was sterilization of the workers. It began to be known Hitler had the same idea.

In desperation, I think, I boldly had two children at the beginning of the Depression. You couldn't get any other kind of life, and you might give birth to friends and allies. I had two girls, who all my life, have been just that.

I became a correspondent from the Middle West, reporting on the farmers' struggles, the third party, all that was happening. I wrote for several national magazines and began to have stories in *American Mercury*, and university quarterlies, and writings about my children were sold to the women's magazines. So I began to make a modest living at writing, which was wonderful. I became known as a witness, as I wanted to be. I became well known for two pieces: *Corn Village*, about the small town; and, *I Was Marching*, about the '34 teamsters' strike.

I feel we must be deeply rooted in the tribal family and in the social community. This is becoming a strong and beautiful force now in our societies. Women speaking out boldly, going to jail for peace and sanctuary, defending the children against hunger. We still get half of what men get. But as I saw in Nairobi the struggle of women is now global. My Gramma and mother are not any more silenced and alone. Writing has become with women not a concealment, but an illumination. We are not alone. The hundreds of women writers now who speak for us to a large audience.

This makes me write more than I ever did. I have 140 notebooks, my letter to the world, published some day for a new woman I dreamed of. I have 24 great grandchildren who have freedoms I could only dream of. One granddaughter is raising five children herself. Another has two sons. They are not alone; that's the point. They live in collectives and work in social fields with women and children. They have an independence I never had, a boldness and a communal life and support.

I am writing as I never wrote before. I have three books, besides my notebooks, to "finish." I call it getting in my crop before the frost! It is my best writing, I believe...I have learned to bear witness with love and compassion and warm readers to whom I am truthful. And they return my witness, so women rise from the darkness singing together, not the small and tortured chorus of my grandmothers, but millions becoming visible and singing.

THE AUTHOR

MAUREEN R. MICHELSON founded NewSage Press in 1985. Her background is in journalism, having worked as a news reporter for *Time* magazine, an editor of an international arts magazine, and 18 years as a professional writer and editor. Michelson has also authored three books. NewSage Press has received national attention for its quality books. Several titles have been nominated or selected by the American Library Association as "Best Books for Young Adults," including the first edition of *Women & Work*.

OTHER BOOKS BY NEWSAGE PRESS

Blue Moon over Thurman Street
   by Ursula K. Le Guin and Roger Dorband

The C-Word: Teenagers and Their Families Living with Cancer
   by Elena Dorfman

When the Bough Breaks: Pregnancy and the Legacy of Addiction
   by Kira Corser and Frances Payne Adler

A Portrait of American Mothers & Daughters
   by Raisa Fastman

Organizing for Our Lives: New Voices from Rural Communities
   by Richard Steven Street and Samuel Orozco; Foreword by Cesar Chavez

Family Portraits in Changing Times
   by Helen Nestor

Stories of Adoption: Loss & Reunion
   by Eric Blau

Common Heroes: Facing a Life Threatening Illness
   by Eric Blau

The New Americans: Immigrant Life in Southern California
   by Ulli Steltzer

Exposures: Women and Their Art
   by Betty Ann Brown and Arlene Raven, Photographs by Kenna Love

For a NewSage Press catalog, write or call:
NewSage Press
PO Box 607, Troutdale, OR 97060

503-695-2211: (Fax) 503-695-5406